Annie Bell's Vegetable Book

Also by Annie Bell

A Feast of Flavours
Evergreen

Annie Bell's
Vegetable Book

Photographs by Lisa Linder

MICHAEL JOSEPH
LONDON

MICHAEL JOSEPH LTD

Published by the Penguin Group
27 Wrights Lane, London w8 5tz
Viking Penguin Inc., 375 Hudson Street, New York, New York 10014, USA
Penguin Books Australia Ltd, Ringwood, Victoria, Australia
Penguin Books Canada Ltd, 10 Alcorn Avenue, Toronto, Ontario, Canada m4v 3b2
Penguin Books (NZ) Ltd, 182–190 Wairau Road, Auckland 10, New Zealand

Penguin Books Ltd, Registered Offices: Harmondsworth, Middlesex, England

First published in Great Britain 1997
10 9 8 7 6 5 4 3 2 1

Set in 11.5/14pt Monotype Centaur
Designed in QuarkXpress on an Apple Macintosh
Printed and bound by Hunter & Foulis Ltd

A CIP catalogue record for this book is available from the British Library

ISBN 07181 4080 X

The moral right of the author has been asserted

With thanks to: Maryse Boxer Design at Joseph Maison
26 Sloane Street, London, sw1 for china, glass and accessories;
Josiah Wedgwood & Sons Ltd for the use of their Wedgwood
Traditional Plain Shape Queensware

For my parents

Contents

Introduction

For as long as I can remember I have loved eating vegetables. As a child it was a fairly narrow spectrum of dishes that took in ratatouille and cauliflower cheese, with more exotic fare when we went on holiday to Italy or Southern France. In my eyes these were the special treats in life, and as I have grown older vegetables have remained the real stars of the kitchen.

I have never understood why a piece of meat should be glorified, with vegetables playing second fiddle, when I would far rather it was the other way around. Collectively vegetables present the most magical array of textures, flavours, aromas and colours that can be handled and combined in any number of different ways, often resulting in something completely new. Such cookery is very much in its infancy having been ignored, certainly within our own culture.

Obviously if the concentration is on using vegetables rather than meat the result is going to be vegetarian, although this is more a byproduct of this book than being one of the over-riding aims. All the recipes are vegetarian, but I haven't excluded the mention of meat and fish within the text because I hope the book will have a much broader appeal.

In looking at vegetarianism today it is apparent that it has thrown off its brown rice and lentils image and declared itself a new style of cooking. But even so, sadly most of what is around is every bit as dreary as what's been left behind. I think it's a case of trying too hard to be creative. In order to make the food seem more interesting or exciting, so many herbs, flavourings and ingredients are combined, that the end result is a bit of a mess. I suppose I feel there is a need for more clarity and restraint.

Equally I increasingly shy away from the notion of three different things going on at once on a plate. Is it a fear of being boring that deters people from serving a whole cauliflower in a creamy almond sauce, an unctuous mass of warm sliced potatoes and onions sautéed in olive oil, or stoved Jerusalem artichokes scented with Provençal herbs as dishes in their own right rather than as one of several accompanying vegetable dishes?

It's a spillover from the idea that if you have a piece of meat or fish you need to have a carbohydrate such as potatoes to go with it, as well as two vegetables. So that when a quiche is served, even when vegetarian, it comes with accompanying potatoes and two 'interesting' salads, when in reality it would be much more pleasurable to first eat the quiche and then enjoy the salads.

It has a lot to do with our Northern European culture; whereas the Italians make a celebration about serving a single vegetable as it is, or a piece of fish without the dancing attendance of side dishes. And the rice, pasta or gnocchi come in between, again on their own.

I find the best vegetarian food around exists within a cultural setting, be it Lebanese, Italian or Provençal, and studying such cookery has provided me with endless inspiration. I wanted to concentrate on what I enjoyed about each vegetable rather than the omission of meat, and these are fine examples to follow.

In choosing the selection of vegetables, first off I indulged with a list of my favourites like avocados, aubergines and spinach, followed by the ones like carrots and cabbages that are always around, and finally a handful of less usual vegetables that cooks might get stuck on, such as horseradish and samphire.

As much for my own convenience as yours, every vegetable has at least one recipe that takes 30 minutes or under, and these have been graded as 'fast'. I can think of a million reasons why time can be the most important consideration. For myself it is the early evening rush between finishing work, bathing my son and trying to assemble dinner at the same time. But likewise some of the recipes are more obviously intended for occasions such as

entertaining, when you might want to spend a little more time cooking. I am thinking of an asparagus quiche, wild mushroom cassoulet, or peperonata with Parmesan shortbread – not that such food is technically difficult, it's just more enjoyable to cook when you can go about it in a leisurely fashion.

The list of 'ideas' for cooking each vegetable are simply ways I think would work well, combinations of ingredients that I like together, and if I had a supply of that vegetable to hand this is how I would think of using it. I would hope the ideas have a modern feel; just about everyone carries soy sauce, sesame oil and the like in their larder these days as well as standard Western ingredients.

I am sufficiently old-fashioned to take pleasure in eating produce that is in season. But as you may have noticed, the 'seasons' for vegetables seem to be for ever growing longer. This isn't the result of global warming, but because in order to compete with imports, new varieties that can cope with the weather are being developed, as are new techniques for extending the growing season. But despite this stretching there are still periods when vegetables are plentiful and inexpensive, and very obviously 'in season'.

My main reservations about imports are environmental: if at all possible, dragging food from one part of the world to another is to be avoided. But to say categorically that vegetables are not as fresh if they come from another country would be unfair. Equally it is difficult to say that English asparagus is going to be better than South African or Spanish. This may be the case the majority of the time, but given that quality varies within any country it makes blanket generalizations dangerous.

For the vegetable connoisseur one of the great areas of interest lies with variety, a luxury of being able to grow your own. Country house hotels and restaurants often have enviable gardens, the finest I have visited being Raymond Blanc's at Le Manoir aux Quat' Saisons, where he says he tasted his way through about twenty-four varieties of any one vegetable before deciding which one he should grow. Things are definitely improving variety-wise in the shops, albeit they're far from perfect. Roll on the day when it will be law to label every vegetable with its variety so that consumers will have the opportunity to taste and develop their own likes and dislikes, as we already do with apples and potatoes for instance.

The best advice I can give on shopping is to rely on suppliers that you trust. I am fortunate to have a wonderful greengrocer close by whom I trust every bit as much as I do the cheesemonger or the French patisserie. Shopping there is very personalized and you are asked by whoever is serving what size you want, when do you want to eat the produce and how are you cooking it, before they select it by hand and pop it into a brown paper bag for weighing.

I do, whenever possible, buy organic produce, which is less than half the time if I am honest. Although it does finally seem to be coming in from the cold and filtering into mainstream shops. More and more cooks are coming round to the idea of organic as being the very best in quality. And there's an elemental pleasure in knowing that a vegetable has been naturally grown without any chemical interference; it's immensely satisfying to arrive home from a shopping trip with a bag full of different organic produce.

I hope you will derive as much enjoyment from cooking these recipes as I did in making them up. I'm still quite happy to settle down to a plate of ratatouille or cauliflower cheese, but it's nice to know there are a hundred and one alternatives that are just as delicious.

Food Notes

Olive Oil

I keep three types of olive oil to hand. First, I keep an inexpensive extra virgin olive oil for cooking with. Second, an estate-bottled oil for using uncooked in dishes – salads especially – and for pouring over cooked vegetable dishes. I have a particular fondness for Sicilian and Ligurian oils, which are very elegant and fragrant, not overly peppery. And last, I keep a pure olive oil, again for cooking with, and for making mayonnaise.

Vegetable Stock

Sometimes in recipes I have suggested a 'double-strength' vegetable stock. This is because I always keep several half-pint cartons of bought fresh stock in the freezer rather than making my own, and these come in 'double-strength'. To make your own, prepare an ordinary stock and reduce it by half by boiling it.

To make a basic stock, sweat some chopped onion, leek, carrot, celery, fennel, aubergine, celeriac and courgette in butter or olive oil for about 10 minutes. You can also include some lentils, whole cloves of garlic, herbs, salt and white peppercorns. Cover with water and simmer for 35–45 minutes, skimming as necessary, then strain the stock and reserve it. You can skim off any surface fat once it is cool.

Oven

All these recipes have been tested using a fan-assisted electric oven. I have also given temperatures for ordinary ovens, given that they are not as powerful.

But please use the cooking times for guidance only, because ovens behave in very different ways, and it's much better to whip a tart or gratin out when you think it's cooked rather than leaving it in for the full length of time 'because the recipe says so'.

It's also worth remembering that if you have any baking sheets lying idle in the oven they will affect the circulation of air and the temperature, just as the number of dishes in the oven will do.

Artichokes

Once, when I was out picking wild mushrooms, my companion hacked off a thistle in a field, pared the stem and offered it to me to chew, which took me by surprise. However, hunters once used the stems of thistles to assuage thirst. Thistle flowerheads, which is what artichokes are, do not at the outset sound terribly appetizing, and yet they are considered to be one of the greatest delicacies among vegetables. These, together with wild mushrooms and asparagus, form the basis of special treats for vegetarians. It is the base or heart of the artichoke that we eat, an extension of the stem, and the fleshy pads at the bottom of the leaves or bracts. The hairy and appropriately named choke, which has to be removed before the artichoke is eaten, consists of flowerets which will bloom a spectacular mauve if allowed to do so.

The Romans knew artichokes as *carduus*, and they are indeed related to the cardoon. They were also called *cynara*, after a beautiful maiden who upset a god on Zinara in the Aegean Sea, and was turned into a thistle by him. More scientifically, cynarin is the name of the compound in artichokes that acts to make other foods taste sweet by blocking receptors. When tucking into artichokes it is not the time to produce your finest wine.

These beautiful heads vary from green through to purple, and can be eaten at various stages of maturity. The small heads no larger than an egg, of which I am especially fond, are becoming more popular in this country, although unfortunately they remain expensive. These in fact come from the same plant as the large heads, forming satellites beneath the main stem. Rather curiously, Giacomo Castelvetro says in *The Fruit, Herbs and Vegetables of Italy* (1614) that at one time the English were fortunate enough to have these all year around. What happened?

It must be the effect of cynarin on the palate that leaves one crying out for lemon juice or vinegar. I do not think artichokes in mayonnaise work nearly as well as preparations which offer some sort of acidity, be it only tomato. They also call for a certain richness and succulence within other ingredients.

Selection

When selecting artichokes there is a golden rule: a tightly closed head. If the leaves are beginning to open, they are past their best. They also benefit from a 20-minute soak upside down in a sink of salted water, which will kill off any bugs trapped between their scaly leaves.

Preparation

Lemon juice and vinegar will both nullify the effects of tannic acid, which not only stains your hands but discolours the cut areas of the artichoke flesh when it is exposed to air. Either acidulate a bowl of water with a good slug of lemon juice or of vinegar, or use them neat – dipping the cut areas of the artichokes as you are preparing them, and reserving them in the acidulated water until they are ready for cooking. You will also need to acidulate the water in which they are to be boiled.

Preparing tiny artichokes the size of an egg is no more irksome than peeling a Brussels sprout: they can be eaten choke and all. Simply slice off the bottom, cut away the outside leaves and slice off the top, at which point they will be no larger than a closed rosebud. (Observe the guidelines above for acidulation.) On the continent I have often eaten artichokes of a middling size, somewhere between the large and baby ones. These are usually eaten with about 5 cm/2 inches of stem attached, which will have been peeled. Sadly, I have never come across these here.

Large artichokes require a procedure known as turning. Equip yourself with a small, sharp knife and some acidulated water, and as debris accumulates rather quickly it is a good

idea to have a bin close by. Break the stalk off the base of the artichoke; this should remove some of the tough fibres. Starting at the base, cut away the coarse exterior, dipping the exposed flesh in the acidulated water as you work to prevent it from discolouring. Once you have cut around the sides, slice off the top to about 1 cm/$\frac{1}{2}$ inch above the choke. Reserve the artichokes in the acidulated water.

There are two ways of tackling the choke. It can be removed before cooking, using a knife, and the pitted layer where the choke was rooted to the heart can be scraped away using a teaspoon. I find this is quite a headache, although Joel Robuchon, former chef of the Michelin three-starred restaurant Le Jamin in Paris, maintains that the heart remains whiter. Wherever possible I prefer to cook the artichokes first, then remove the inner leaves and the choke.

Cooking

As a general rule artichokes do need cooking, though Giacomo Castelvetro observes that 'about the size of a walnut they are good raw, with just salt, pepper and some mature cheese to bring out the flavour', and I would add olive oil to his list, having trimmed and finely sliced them. He adds that 'artichokes are not so good to eat raw when they have grown as big as apples'. Quite so.

Bring a large pan of water to the boil and acidulate it with a slug of lemon juice or vinegar – if you have been dipping the artichokes into neat liquor, use this. Boil the hearts for 20 minutes. You should be able to insert a knife into the base with ease. Reserve them in a sink of cold water.

Pull out the inner artichoke leaves, cut out the choke, and use a teaspoon to scrape off the pitted layer. Trim the base and sides of the heart so it is tidy.

The answer to artichoke vinaigrette

Eating a whole artichoke with vinaigrette or melted butter is not to be sniffed at – deliciously idle time spent nibbling at the fleshy base of the leaves before devouring the heart. But there is no getting away from the fact that it is both messy and laborious. A compromise that allows the diner to have his cake and eat it too is to remove the tough base and outside leaves of the artichokes then boil them. When they are cool, pull off and discard any tough-looking leaves, then, holding the artichoke heart, pull off the leaves so that they remain intact as a cone, by working around the choke to loosen them where they join the heart. Pull out any thin central leaves from inside the cone and discard these. Remove the choke, scrape off the pitted layer, and tidy the heart. Serve the cone of leaves beside it.

Artichoke Hearts Filled with Avocado Purée – Shallot Vinaigrette

Artichoke hearts were never designed to be eaten by the bucketful. One artichoke each makes a delicious first course, and 2 with bread would do nicely for lunch.

Prepare the artichokes and cook in acidulated water as described on page 2, leaving the choke in place. Cool them in cold water, then remove the leaves and choke and cut off and reserve the fleshy tips of the leaves. Place these in a liquidizer with the avocado flesh, the tablespoon of lemon juice, the yoghurt and seasoning and reduce to a thick mousse-like purée, adding a drop of milk if necessary.

To make the dressing, whisk the vinegar with salt and pepper, add the olive oil, and stir in the shallot.

To serve, place the artichoke hearts on plates, fill the centre with the avocado purée, and spoon over the vinaigrette.

Photograph opposite page 32.

Serves 2–4

4 large globe artichokes
juice of 1 lemon or vinegar for acidulating water
1 large avocado
1 tablespoon lemon juice
2 tablespoons plain yoghurt
sea salt and freshly ground black pepper

Dressing
1 dessertspoon balsamic vinegar
sea salt and freshly ground black pepper
4 tablespoons extra virgin olive oil
1 heaped dessertspoon finely chopped shallot

Artichoke Fritters with Tartare Sauce

Just about anything deep-fried in batter and dipped into tartare sauce tastes good. Baby artichokes – well, they're a real treat. I like some sprigs of watercress on the side.

To prepare the batter, whisk the flour, salt, beer, egg yolk and olive oil in a bowl. Leave to rest for 20 minutes. When ready to cook the fritters, stiffly whisk the egg white and fold it into the batter.

To make the tartare sauce, whisk the egg yolks and mustard in a bowl, and gradually whisk in the oil to make a mayonnaise: by the end it should be too thick to whisk. Add a good squeeze of lemon juice, then the remainder of the ingredients.

Acidulate a bowl of water with half the lemon juice and bring a large pan of water to the boil with the remaining half. Cut off the base of the artichokes, removing no more than is necessary otherwise they will fall to pieces, then peel away any tough outer leaves and slice off the top so you are left with something resembling a rosebud: reserve these in the bowl of acidulated water, then boil for 7 minutes. Drain and reserve.

Heat the oil to 190°C/375°F in a wok or a deep frying pan, using a jam thermometer to gauge the temperature. Dip the artichokes into the batter and deep-fry them until they are a deep gold, in batches so as not to overcrowd the pan. Allow the oil to come back up to temperature between each batch. Drain on kitchen paper and serve straight away with the tartare sauce.

Serves 4

juice of 1 lemon
900 g/2 lb baby artichokes
groundnut oil for deep-frying

Batter
70 g/2½ oz plain flour
½ teaspoon sea salt
100 ml/3½ fl oz beer
1 medium egg, separated
1 tablespoon extra virgin olive oil

Tartare sauce
2 medium egg yolks
1 teaspoon grainy mustard
350 ml/12 fl oz groundnut oil
squeeze of lemon juice
1 heaped tablespoon finely chopped
    gherkins
1 heaped tablespoon finely chopped capers
1 heaped tablespoon finely chopped flat-
    leaved parsley

Gratin of Artichoke Hearts with Broad Beans

Here warm artichoke hearts are filled with broad beans and tomato in a creamy sauce, which is glazed under the grill.

    To prepare the artichokes, acidulate a large bowl of water with half the lemon juice, and bring a large pan of water to the boil with the remainder. Break off the stem of each artichoke and pare the base and side leaves with a small, sharp knife, dipping the exposed flesh into the acidulated water as you work to prevent it from discolouring. You should have a bud like a closed peony at the top, leaving the choke in place: reserve in the acidulated water. Boil these for 20 minutes – when they are ready a knife should enter the base with ease. Cool them in a sink of cold water.

    While the artichokes are cooking, shell the broad beans. Bring a large pan of water to the boil, add the beans, bring back to the boil, and cook for 5 minutes until tender. Drain the beans and cool in cold water.

    To serve the gratin, preheat the oven to 180°C fan oven/190°C or 375°F electric oven/Gas 5. Whisk the cream till it is semi-stiff and blend in the remaining mustard cream ingredients. Drain the artichoke hearts and remove the upper leaves and the choke, using a knife to loosen it. Scrape off the pitted layer with a teaspoon and tidy the sides. Place these in a shallow gratin dish and season.

    Drain the broad beans and pile on top of the artichokes together with the diced tomato, allowing them to spill over the sides. Spoon the mustard cream over the top and place in the preheated oven for 12 minutes, then under a hot grill until the surface browns in patches. Serve straight away.

Serves 2–4

juice of 1 lemon
4 globe artichokes
200 g/7 oz freshly shelled broad beans
   (700–900 g/1 lb 9 oz–2 lb unshelled)
1 × 200 g/7 oz beefsteak tomato, peeled,
   seeded and diced

Mustard cream
150 ml/5 fl oz double cream
1 rounded teaspoon mild grainy mustard
¼ teaspoon finely grated lemon zest
1 teaspoon lemon juice
1 medium egg yolk
sea salt and freshly ground black pepper

Salad of Baby Artichokes and Parmesan

I love the clean simplicity of this salad – it makes a very nice starter. The artichokes should ideally be the size of an egg. If they are any larger then cut them open and if the choke is visible as fine hairs, nick it out. This is not really a salad that can be tried with larger specimens.

Pare the artichokes as though preparing a Brussels sprout: slice off the base, cut away the tough outer leaves at the sides and slice off the top. Finely slice the remaining part of the artichoke and toss with the lemon juice. Prepare the rest of the artichokes likewise. If you want you can prepare these about an hour in advance – the lemon juice will prevent any discoloration.

Drain off the lemon juice and rinse the sliced artichokes in a sieve. Return to the bowl and season. Arrange the sliced artichokes and Parmesan on a plate and pour over the olive oil.

Serves 4

10 baby artichokes
juice of 1 lemon
sea salt and freshly ground black pepper
50 g/2 oz Parmesan, finely shaved
4 tablespoons extra virgin olive oil

Other Ideas

➤ Serve cooked artichoke hearts with a plain dressing of balsamic vinegar and extra virgin olive oil, made with a large pinch of sugar and a dab of Dijon mustard.

➤ Use Seville orange juice, or a blend of orange and lemon juice, in lieu of vinegar in the dressing, and add lots of chopped herbs.

➤ Make mushrooms à la grècque, add wedges of cooked artichoke heart, and lots of lemon juice, lemon zest and chopped thyme to the liquor. Baby artichokes à la grècque also make a very elegant starter.

➤ Embellish a dressed artichoke heart with black olives and diced tomato, or finely diced white of egg and sieved yolk.

➤ Select gutsy, accompanying leaves for a salad containing cooked artichoke hearts – rocket and watercress, for example, or maybe a little radicchio or chicory.

➤ Artichoke soup is heavenly – cream of, that is.

➤ Make a chunky salad of whole cooked young vegetables in a herbed vinaigrette, including some baby artichokes.

➤ Sauté sliced baby artichokes in olive oil with a little garlic, and add some mushrooms after a couple of minutes. Scatter with chopped parsley. This would be nice with scrambled eggs.

Asparagus

Asparagus

The Greeks loved it, the Romans loved it, and it's been the pride of the vegetable garden since Renaissance times. Certainly it is quite extraordinary: spears which break through the earth from their complex underground crown of roots and buds. It's no doddle to grow – it takes three years to prepare a bed before you can enjoy your first crop, and these must be carefully earthed up, mulched and harvested by hand.

Asparagus tends to be treated with the reverence reserved for really special foods. And it is special – though not always, as anyone who has experienced tasteless jumbo spears will be able to confirm. That it is considered to be such a delicacy is a problem in itself: often it is seen as sacrilege to serve it in any way other than simply boiled, with a butter sauce, and for the finest specimens this is hard to beat. But there are any number of other ways of eating asparagus, and to chargrill and smother it in shavings of Parmesan is just as easy and just as delicious.

There are many different varieties of asparagus: white, purple and the green beloved of the British. In France there is a green variety called 'Lauris', grown in the south, which is considered to be the finest, and the French are also very fond of white asparagus. This comes at a premium, but I am inclined to agree that those tender white spears streaked with violet can be quite superb. I am not, however, a huge fan of the thin asparagus sprue, which rarely has the flavour of the thicker spears.

Wild asparagus has been enjoying something of a vogue recently, a Med-led trend, fine, curly hop-like shoots which are faintly bitter and are delicious served with scrambled eggs or in an omelette. Like most wild vegetables it remains the domain of upmarket greengrocers.

Selection

The main point when buying any type of asparagus is that the scales on the tips should be tightly closed, and the spears should be firm. It is easy enough to tell how fresh it is just by looking at it.

Preparation

When asparagus is thin it should not need peeling – just slice it where it becomes visibly tough and white. When it is finger-thick, slice it where it becomes tough and peel it to within 2 cm/1 inch of the base of the tip, using a potato peeler.

Cooking

When it comes to cooking asparagus there are two myths to be dispensed with. The first is that it should be cooked for 15–20 minutes. On average I cook spears for 5 minutes, which is ample, and the wild asparagus and thin sprue take even less time. The second myth is that an asparagus pan is necessary to achieve spears that are cooked equally at the bottom and at the top. I suspect that these pans derive from the days when spears were given a routine 20 minutes rolling boil, by which time the tips would indeed have disintegrated. An asparagus pan is one more saucepan to store, with limited usage, and an ordinary saucepan will do perfectly well.

Asparagus is not a vegetable that benefits from long, slow braising. Little can improve upon boiling it to preserve its colour and catch it at just the correct moment of tenderness. Chargrilled asparagus, however, is excellent. Paint it with olive oil, season and then grill it, and serve with shavings of Parmesan and rocket leaves. It is also good roasted.

There are two ways of boiling asparagus: either cook the spears loose, or arrange them in a bundle with the tips all pointing in the same direction. I see no need to cut all the spears the same length – you just end up wasting good asparagus. Tie a length of string firmly around the bundle, starting at the top and wrapping it spiralling first downwards, then back up to the top

again. Tie the ends in a knot and cut. This method also makes it simple to remove the asparagus from the pan.

Bring a large pan of salted water to the boil. Thin asparagus will take about 3 minutes, finger-thick asparagus will take 4–5 minutes. If the asparagus is loose, I remove a spear and cut a small slice off the thick end to test – if it slices with ease, it is cooked. If cooking it in a bundle, lift the end out of the water and insert a knife into a spear. If it meets with little resistance it is cooked. Either drain the asparagus into a sieve if cooking it loose, or remove the bundle with tongs and place it on a tea-towel to drain thoroughly – there is little worse than sitting down to a plate of watery vegetables.

If you are serving it hot, pour the sauce straight over. If you are serving it cold, plunge it into a sink of cold water to cool it, which will preserve its colour – you will, however, lose a little flavour on the way.

Trimmings

Delicious sauces and soups can be founded on asparagus trimmings: keep any peelings and finely slice the tough end that is usually discarded, starting at the cut edge and slicing until it becomes really woody, which may be the last 1–2.5 cm/^{1}/$_2$–1 inch of each spear.

Sweat the slices in butter with some finely chopped shallot, cover with vegetable stock and braise for 5 minutes, then liquidize and pass through a sieve. Enrich this purée with crème fraîche or double cream and you have an asparagus sauce, or thin it further for a soup. If you are making an asparagus tart or a gratin, combine the purée with the cream, whole egg and egg yolks when you make the custard.

Asparagus Quiche

To prepare the pastry, mix together the egg yolk, sugar, salt and water. Rub the butter into the flour (you can use a food processor). Bring the dough together with the egg and water solution and knead it for a few minutes, then wrap it in clingfilm and rest it in the fridge for 45 minutes.

Heat the oven to 190°C fan oven/200°C or 400°F electric oven/Gas 6. Lightly flour a work surface, roll the pastry 0.25 cm/⅛ inch thick, and use to line a 23 cm/9 inch tart case 3.5 cm/1½ inches deep with a removable base. Trim the top, cover the pastry case with foil or baking parchment and baking beans (I use dried pulses), and bake for 15 minutes. Remove the foil and beans and cook for another 5 minutes until just starting to colour.

While the pastry is baking, bring a pan of salted water to the boil. Trim the asparagus where it becomes visibly tough and halve the spears. Boil them for 3 minutes, drain and reserve. Whisk together the egg, egg yolks, milk and cream, season and stir in half the grated Parmesan.

Arrange the asparagus on the base of the tart case, pour the custard over and sprinkle with the remaining grated Parmesan. Bake for about 30 minutes, until the custard is set and the surface is nicely golden. Eat warm or cold.

Serves 4–6

Pastry
1 medium egg yolk
½ teaspoon caster sugar
½ teaspoon sea salt
65 ml/2½ fl oz water
70 g/2½ oz unsalted butter, diced
250 g/9 oz plain flour, sifted

Filling
350 g/12 oz finger-thick asparagus
1 medium egg, plus 2 egg yolks
200 ml/7 fl oz milk
200 ml/7 fl oz double cream
sea salt and freshly ground black pepper
60 g/2 oz grated Parmesan

Griddled Brochettes of Asparagus

These look wonderful, a neat row of spears lined up on a skewer and grilled. Eaten with soy sauce and sesame seeds, this is asparagus at its plainest, and it makes a change from the 'with butter' scenario. Keep these in mind when the barbecue season approaches.

Trim the asparagus spears where they become visibly woody, and stick them on to 4 metal skewers. Heat a griddle over a low heat. You will need one that covers two rings if you want to cook them in one go – but there is nothing to stop you doing them in batches and serving the asparagus at room temperature.

Paint the brochettes with olive oil and season with freshly ground black pepper, then grill for 5–7 minutes each side until nicely charred. Serve with a few drops of soy sauce and a scattering of sesame seeds.

Serves 4

800 g/1¾ lb finger-thick asparagus
extra virgin olive oil for grilling
freshly ground black pepper

To serve
dark soy sauce
toasted sesame seeds

Other Ideas

➤ Make a salad of asparagus and sliced avocado with toasted sesame seeds and dress with lime juice, balsamic vinegar and extra virgin olive oil.

➤ Serve warm asparagus smothered in melted butter, and scattered with breadcrumbs fried until crisp, seasoned with thyme, lemon zest and chilli.

➤ Asparagus and morel mushrooms are a serious treat in unison: cook the asparagus, then sauté the morels in clarified butter and add the asparagus to the pan to heat through. You could also add a little cream and simmer for a minute or two to make a sauce.

➤ For a really light hollandaise, make a sabayon base by whisking egg yolks with a little white wine in a bowl over a saucepan of simmering water until frothy, then whisk in the melted butter until you have a thick, creamy sauce.

➤ Make a firm polenta, cut it into cubes, and chargrill. Mix with cooked asparagus and peas and dress with olive oil and shredded basil leaves.

➤ Thinly slice cooked asparagus, mix it with cooked red rice and lots of freshly chopped herbs, and dress with lemon juice and extra virgin olive oil.

See also:

Puff Pastry Tart with Asparagus and Horseradish (page 98)

Aubergines

Effortlessly perfect, did nature really provide such a blemish-free skin, as taut and glossy as that of an aubergine? If you habitually delve into oriental delis then you are probably used to coming across aubergines in a variety of forms: small white Easter eggs, long fingers, finely striped types and diminutive pea-green affairs. And of course there are the bog-standard purple aubergines about the length of your hand. Having never had any great success with the small aubergines, I will stick to the ones I know and love: the large purple ones, including, if I happen to come across them, those that are purple streaked with ivory, which have an extremely good flavour and can be treated in exactly the same way.

Aubergines are often seen as the answer to the meatless meal: stuff 'em, roast 'em, bake 'em, they are large enough when embellished to qualify as a main course, and there is something about the texture of the flesh which lends them to this substitution. The actual flavour is fairly bland, but this is a part of their versatility: they will absorb spices, garlic and chillies, marry well with stronger elements like capers, gherkins and freshly chopped herbs, and they are excellent afforded a sweet and sour treatment.

One of their attractions as a meat substitute is the way they grill to a smoky exterior, either blistered over a griddle so that the interior is tainted with smoke, or sliced, brushed with olive oil and seared until the flesh has the charred streaks we welcome in fish or barbecued meat.

When griddled whole, the flesh can be puréed with Greek yoghurt, garlic and a squeeze of lemon, with chopped parsley stirred in. It is not until you hear the name baba ghanoush for about the third time that you actually remember it: the smoky flesh is blended with a light tahini (sesame) paste, and sharpened with lots of lemon juice. A large bowl of one of these purées, some black olives, warm pitta bread, a saucer of olive oil, and perhaps a few toasted nuts and spices pounded together in which to dip, make one of my favourite grazing combinations before dinner.

In salads I think it is best to capitalize on the rich oiliness aubergines acquire when roasted, fried or grilled, and to forget about the vinegar and lemon juice. I'll settle for a few shavings of Parmesan or a young goat's cheese.

Stuffed aubergines

Stuffed aubergines are definitely a cliché, along with omelettes: if you're going to get a bad second course offering as a vegetarian, that'll be it – although there is no need for this to be the case.

There are two ways of approaching the stuffing of an aubergine. Normally I halve them, score the cut surface and rub olive oil over the whole thing, and bake them until they are turning golden. Then you can either cut out the centre and sauté or mix it with whatever ingredients you plan for the stuffing, or make a stuffing with a mixture of brioche crumbs, Gruyère, butter and herbs that blends to a paste, and spread it to cover the surface.

When I want to serve a selection of stuffed vegetables – for instance, aubergine, courgette and mushrooms with a few rocket leaves or watercress – I cut the aubergines into thick rounds and roast these, and then stuff the cut surface. They will also be good baked on top of a tomato sauce.

To salt or not to salt

There are various elements to the salting argument, the foremost being bitterness. Rumours have been circulating for some years now that the bitterness has been bred out of aubergines. Which is not

to say that someone somewhere is not growing good old-fashioned bitter aubergines, but I have stopped salting them in order to extract their juices. Some argue that the juices should be bled because they are indigestible, but again I find that experience does not substantiate this.

And finally, it is said that if you extract the juices the aubergines will not absorb as much oil when you fry them. Well, sorry, but this too I would disagree with, because there is a knack to frying them that limits the amount of oil they drink.

Cooking

A frying aubergine is a real spiv – heed its demands for oil at the beginning of cooking and the end result will be dripping in excess grease. Be firm.

The trick is to ignore the initial cries for more oil when you add the aubergines to the pan. If you are cooking aubergine cubes, heat a few tablespoons of oil in a frying pan and once it is very hot add the raw cubed aubergine, tossing almost constantly for several minutes until it begins to brown. At first it will seem impossibly dry, but as it continues to cook the aubergine's own juices will come to the rescue. Likewise when you are frying or grilling aubergine slices, paint just one side with oil and cook until this is coloured. Then paint the top side with oil, turn and fry or grill this too.

For chargrilling, slice your aubergines as thick as you want, either in round slices or long slipper-shapes the length of the aubergine. As with frying, paint them sparingly with olive oil, grill one side until it is streaked with dark brown and the flesh is translucent, paint the upper side with oil, season this and chargrill.

You can boil aubergines whole and then cook the flesh with sauce ingredients, but this is not a method that appeals to me personally, I prefer roasting. Preheat the oven to 200°C fan oven/220°C or 425°F electric oven/Gas 7 and roast the aubergines for 25–30 minutes until the skins are wrinkled and charred. (Roast them on the grid of a grill pan to collect any juices that may be exuded. If they cook sitting in a pool of their own juices these can burn and flavour the flesh.)

For dips and purées, peel off the skin from the roasted aubergine, place the flesh in a sieve and press out the juices. Then purée the flesh in a food processor with garlic, olive oil, Greek yoghurt, lemon juice, herbs and so forth.

Warm Salad of Roasted Aubergine, Tomatoes and Cannellini Beans

This is a fairly substantial casserole, but it will double up as a first or a main course. You could use haricot beans if cannellini beans are not to be found.

Preheat the oven to 160°C fan oven/170°C or 325°F electric oven/ Gas 3. Cut the aubergine into 5 cm/2 inch rounds and quarter them. Cut a cone from each tomato to remove the core and halve or quarter if large. Arrange the aubergine, tomatoes, chillies and garlic in a roasting dish. Drizzle over the honey and olive oil and season. Roast for 1½ hours, basting occasionally. Discard the chillies, squeeze the garlic cloves from their casing, and transfer the vegetables to a serving dish, leaving the juices in the pan.

You need to cook the soaked beans at the same time as the vegetables. Put them in a flameproof casserole and cover with water by 5 cm/2 inches. Do not add any salt. Bring the beans to the boil on top of the stove and skim any surface foam. Cover the casserole and place in the oven for 1½ hours or until the beans are soft, then drain and mix them in with the roasted vegetables.

Grind the saffron filaments in a pestle and mortar and blend with 1 dessertspoon of boiling water. Stir this into the roasting juices with the red wine vinegar, adjust the seasoning and pour over the vegetables and beans. Scatter over the parsley and serve warmish, or at room temperature.

Serves 4

1 large aubergine (or 2 small)
900 g/2 lb tomatoes (175–200 g/ 6–7 oz each)
2 red chillies
½ a head of garlic, top cut off
1 dessertspoon clear honey
6 tablespoons extra virgin olive oil
sea salt and freshly ground black pepper
175 g/6 oz cannellini beans, soaked overnight
15 saffron filaments
1 dessertspoon red wine vinegar
1 heaped tablespoon flat-leaved parsley, finely chopped

Brioche Sandwich Filled with Aubergine Fritters, Saffron Mayonnaise and Chutney

The line-up is this: toasted brioche spread with saffron mayonnaise and chutney, stashed with aubergine fritters and a little salad of spring onions, coriander and flat-leaved parsley. Porcini mushrooms made into fritters would make a delectable addition, or alternative, to the aubergine.

Any chutney will do, but not too sweet – no Branston's please, that's death by vinegar. You may not want to use all the mayonnaise – save the rest for a potato salad.

To make the batter, whisk together the lager, flour, cumin, seasoning, egg yolk and olive oil and leave to rest for 20 minutes. When ready to cook the fritters, whisk the egg white until stiff and fold into the batter.

To make the saffron mayonnaise, grind the saffron filaments and infuse with 1 dessertspoon of boiling water. Whisk the egg yolk and mustard in a bowl, and gradually whisk in the oil until the mayonnaise is too thick to whisk any further. Add the saffron liquid, which will thin it slightly.

Trim the spring onions and cut into thin strips. Combine with an equal amount of coriander and parsley fronds.

To make the aubergine fritters, heat the oil in a wok or a deep-frying pan to 190°C/375°F, dunk the aubergine slices into the batter, and deep-fry until golden. Remove and drain on kitchen paper. Two batches ought to do it.

While the fritters are cooking, heat the grill and toast the brioche on both sides.

To assemble the sandwiches, spread half the mayonnaise on one slice, spread the chutney on the other, arrange the fritters on the mayonnaise and top with the onion and herbs. Close, halve diagonally, and serve straightaway.

Photograph between pages 32 and 33.

Serves 4

3 spring onions
coriander and flat-leaved parsley fronds
8 slices of unsweetened brioche
1 heaped dessertspoon chutney

Aubergine fritters
125 ml/4 fl oz lager
100 g/3½ oz plain flour
1 level teaspoon ground cumin
sea salt and freshly ground black pepper
1 medium egg, separated
1 tablespoon extra virgin olive oil
groundnut oil for deep-frying
165 g/6 oz aubergine, sliced
   0.75 cm/⅓ inch thick

Saffron mayonnaise
20 saffron filaments
1 medium egg yolk
½ teaspoon Dijon mustard
175–200 ml/6–7 fl oz groundnut oil

Aubergine and Mozzarella Rolls – Pesto Dressing

I have an inkling that Simon Hopkinson, cookery writer on the *Independent*, owns the copyright to aubergines with pesto, a great combination. Here grilled slices of aubergine are rolled around buffalo mozzarella and roasted red pepper, and a pesto dressing spooned over.

Heat the oven to 200°C fan oven/220°C or 425°F electric oven/ Gas 7 and roast the peppers on the grid of a grill pan for 15–20 minutes – the skins should appear loose but not too black. Place the peppers inside a plastic carrier bag, seal and leave them to cool, then skin and deseed them, working over an open plastic bag or a bowl to retain the juices. Slice the peppers into strips.

While the peppers are cooking make the dressing. Toast the pine-nuts in the oven for 4 minutes until lightly golden. Chop the garlic, sprinkle with a little salt and crush to a paste. Place the basil, pine-nuts, olive oil and garlic in a food processor and reduce to a purée, then stir in the cheese, season with black pepper, and add any reserved pepper juices. Cover and chill until required.

Heat a griddle (ridged or flat). Slice the aubergines lengthwise 0.5 cm/¼ inch thick, brush one side with olive oil and grill until charred on the underside. Brush the topside with oil, season, turn and grill this side too. You will not be able to use the end slices in this recipe, but grill them anyway and use them in a salad.

Once all the aubergine slices are cooked and cooled, cut the mozzarellas into elongated chunks – one for each aubergine slice. Place a strip of pepper and a piece of mozzarella inside each aubergine slice and roll it up lengthwise. Serve the rolls with the pesto dressing spooned over.

Serves 4

2 red peppers
2 large aubergines
extra virgin olive oil for grilling
2 buffalo mozzarellas

Dressing
15 g/½ oz pine-nuts
1 garlic clove, peeled
sea salt
60 g/2 oz basil leaves
8 tablespoons extra virgin olive oil
25 g/1 oz freshly grated Parmesan
freshly ground black pepper

Other Ideas

➤ Griddle slices of aubergine and make into a salad with chunks of fresh goat's cheese, diced tomato and chopped mint: pour more olive oil over when serving.

➤ Make a sweet and sour tomato sauce by adding a little sugar and a little vinegar to a basic fresh tomato sauce as you simmer it. Add fried cubes of aubergine, and some raisins and pine-nuts.

➤ Halve aubergines, paint with olive oil and roast them. Serve with pesto and shavings of Parmesan.

➤ Make aubergine caviar with roasted and diced aubergine, chopped shallots, garlic, tomato, olive oil and lemon juice.

➤ Make a gratin of aubergine: layer it with tomato, slivers of garlic and chopped oregano, scatter breadcrumbs over and bake.

➤ Make a mock moussaka with lentils instead of minced lamb, topped with the requisite sliced aubergine and béchamel.

See also:

Aubergine Yam Tart (page 71)
Grilled Aubergine Slices in Ginger Marinade (page 89)
Aubergine Purée (page 99)
Wild Mushroom Cassoulet (page 118)
Aubergines with a Porcini Crust (page 119)

Avocado

This is a fruit, of course, and so shouldn't really be in this book at all, but given that we treat it as a vegetable and that it's one of my favourites, it seems fair to include it.

As a colour, the avocado seems to have been abused: bathroom suites and the colour of the Queen Mum's hat. All very seventies, but since we're enjoying a seventies revival perhaps it's on its way back.

There is nothing like authenticity to improve upon the flavour of something. The only real-life avocado experience I can boast happened in the Caribbean, where my husband and I gorged on the huge green fruits grown on the estate where we were staying: we filled them with crab, ate them with vinaigrette, in sandwiches, in soups, every which way – that lovely lime-green flesh known as poor man's butter in the tropics. We ignored the fact that the very best avocados are not these whoppers at all, with their thin bright green skins and flesh which tends to wateriness. It is the Hass variety that is supreme, with its warty exterior, black when ripe, and dense nutty flesh with hints of hazelnuts and anise. The little cocktail sausage-shaped avos are also good value.

Avocados are the stuff that grand vegetarian sandwiches are made of: granary bread, mustard and cress or alfalfa sprouts, black olives, some hummus or a few slices of creamy Brie or Vacherin Mont d'Or, and lots of buttery slices of avocado. An oatcake with a few slices of avo, a squeeze of lemon and seasoning is another favourite snack. And guacamole comes next on the list – the acidity of lime juice and tomato cuts through the richness as well as preventing it from discolouring: chilli and coriander make up the perfect match.

Selecting and ripening

If you want to eat avocados the same day that you buy them, you will have to make sure you choose ripe ones. Press them gently – those that yield to pressure are suitable for eating straightaway. Most avocados, however, are sold unripe: let them ripen in the fruit bowl and then keep them in the fridge. If you put them in the fridge before they are ripe, nasty black patches and off flavours will develop.

Avocados do not ripen on the tree; they must be harvested for this to happen. But storing them in an airtight bag will prevent them from ripening.

Preparation

A halved avocado filled with prawn cocktail is a delicious cliché, and understandable if you consider how easy it is to prepare. If you do want to serve them halved and filled, cut a small slice off the base to stop them from rolling.

The best way to peel an avocado is to remove it from the stone in two halves, skin on, then cut the skin into quarters and peel it off.

The flesh of avocados discolours on exposure to air, the panacea being a squeeze of lemon juice or vinegar, but even this is only a temporary answer – as anyone who has ever kept an avocado overnight in this fashion knows, they will still be black in the morning and will taste most vile. Nor am I convinced by the stone in the middle of the bowl of avocado purée as a prevention against discoloration. Having long thought this I recently read Harold McGee's debunking of this myth in *The Curious Cook*: you might just as well insert a lightbulb into the centre. That doesn't work either.

Avocado with Tabbouleh and Fried Haloumi

Tabbouleh involves huge amounts of fresh parsley and mint, but the herbal mix is one you can play around with, the important thing being that the herbs are young and tender, and freshly chopped, and the wheat, a silent partner, should be fine brown burghul, added as a smattering after the salad has been mixed. You can also serve this on a large platter – a square one looks good, with the avocado, tabbouleh and fried haloumi arranged in rows.

First make the tabbouleh: rinse the burghul wheat in a fine-mesh sieve and leave it on the side to absorb the remaining moisture. Chop the parsley, holding the bunch and slicing from leaf to stalk. Combine the parsley, tomato, mint and onion in a bowl, add the seasoning, the oil and lemon juice and combine. Mix in the burghul. To keep tabbouleh, seal the surface with a lettuce leaf and cover with clingfilm.

To serve the salad, halve the avocados, remove the stones and skin, and slice into long thin strips. Place a pile of tabbouleh in the centre of 4 plates and lay the avocado around the outside, drizzling the balsamic vinegar and 4 dessertspoons of olive oil over the avocado.

Now cook the haloumi: heat some olive oil in a frying pan (you can either use 2 frying pans or cook the cheese in 2 batches), dredge the haloumi slices in the flour and cook over a medium heat for 2 minutes each side until nicely golden and slightly crispy on the outside. Drain on kitchen paper. Place the fried haloumi on top of the tabbouleh and serve straight away.

Photograph between pages 32 and 33.

Serves 4

Tabbouleh
1½ tablespoons fine burghul
100 g/4 oz bunch of flat-leaved parsley, tough stalks removed
2 standard tomatoes, sliced and then chopped
1 handful of mint leaves, chopped
1 large spring onion, finely sliced and then chopped
1 level teaspoon sea salt
½ teaspoon freshly ground black pepper
3 tablespoons extra virgin olive oil
2 tablespoons lemon juice

Avocados
3 small ripe avocados
4 teaspoons balsamic vinegar
4 dessertspoons extra virgin olive oil

Fried haloumi
olive oil for frying
225 g/8 oz haloumi cheese, cut into 8 slices
plain flour for dredging

Avocado with Double Tomato Sauce

I first tasted a version of this sauce at Château de Saran — Moët et Chandon's hospitality château in Champagne — where the sun-dried tomatoes were billed as 'confit de tomates'.

The sauce is also delicious spooned over whole buffalo mozzarellas or served as a base for grilled red mullet fillets.

Bring a pan of water to the boil. Cut a cone from the top of each tomato to remove the core, plunge them into the boiling water for 20 seconds and then into a sink of cold water. Slip off the skins, halve and scoop out the seeds, and cut the flesh into 0.5 cm/¼ inch dice.

Place the diced plum tomatoes in a bowl and sprinkle over the sugar and salt; leave for 30 minutes to exude the juices, then stir in the olive oil, sun-dried tomatoes and shallot and season with pepper.

Just before serving, incise the avocado skin into quarters and peel it off. Now remove the flesh in 2 halves. Cover the base of 4 plates with the sauce and place 2 halves of avocado on each, domed side upwards.

Serves 4

4 thin-skinned avocados

Sauce
800 g/1¾ lb plum tomatoes
1 level teaspoon caster sugar
1 level teaspoon sea salt
4 tablespoons extra virgin olive oil
60 g/2 oz sun-dried tomatoes in oil, finely chopped
1 heaped tablespoon finely chopped shallot
freshly ground black pepper

Avocado-stuffed Avocados

A spot of minimalism: halves of avocado filled with an avocado mousse. You are likely to have a bit of extra mousse, so this could stretch to feed 6 if you buy an extra avocado.

Halve 2 of the avocados and scoop out the flesh. Place in a liquidizer with the lemon juice, Tabasco, fromage frais and seasoning, reduce to a purée, then pass through a sieve. Whip the cream and fold into the mousse.

Halve the 2 remaining avocados and remove the stones (if you like, take a thin slice off each base to stop them rolling around on the plate), then season the cut surface and fill generously with the mousse.

Heat the olive oil in a small frying pan. Add the seeds – they will sizzle and turn crisp almost immediately – then add the balsamic vinegar, which will splutter. Spoon the hot oil over the avocados and serve straight away.

Serves 4

4 Hass avocados
2 tablespoons lemon juice
a few drops of Tabasco
3 heaped tablespoons fromage frais
sea salt and freshly ground black pepper
50 ml/2 fl oz double cream

Spice oil
2 tablespoons extra virgin olive oil
½ teaspoon cumin seeds, crushed
½ teaspoon coriander seeds, crushed
1 dessertspoon balsamic vinegar

Tomato, Avocado and Basil Salad

Making a good tomato salad deserves care and attention. It is, without any doubt, my favourite salad, plain or variation thereof.

Having procured your selection of tomatoes, either slice them if they're of the slicing size, or halve or quarter them, a serrated knife is specially made for the job.

The next step is to 'bleed' them of some of their juices, which takes the place of any vinegar – tomatoes are much too delicate to be soused and they have their own acidity, so it really isn't necessary. Sprinkle them with salt, caster sugar and freshly ground black pepper and leave them for 15–30 minutes, by which time their juices will be running.

At its most basic, you can at this point drown them in extra virgin olive oil. The next step is to tuck some shredded basil leaves in here and there. Buffalo mozzarella (the real one) was designed for sitting in thick slices beneath a juicy pile of tomatoes. Anchovies and avocado are my other two favourite partners. Herbs beyond basil? Not without offending the tomatoes.

This recipe is for one of my favourite combinations: tomatoes and avocados, with a few salty olives thrown in. It would be nothing without a large chunk of crusty bread for mopping up the juices, and there should be a lot of juices, in fact you can leave the tomatoes to bleed for up to an hour, by which time you will have a lovely soupy pool to dip into.

Cherry tomatoes excepted, cut out the core then halve, quarter or slice the tomatoes as seems appropriate. Place in a bowl, sprinkle with the salt, sugar and black pepper and leave for 30 minutes.

There is a knack to preparing avocados so that the flesh doesn't go mushy: quarter and remove from the stone, then peel off the skin and cut the flesh into long slivers. Arrange the avocado, tomatoes, shreds of basil and olives together on a large plate, shallow rather than deep, and pour over the olive oil. Decorate with a few tiny leaves of basil.

Serves 4

700 g/1 lb 9 oz assorted tomatoes
$^{3}/_{4}$ teaspoon sea salt
$^{1}/_{2}$ teaspoon caster sugar
freshly ground black pepper
2 avocados
1 teaspoon finely shredded basil leaves
100 g/3$^{1}/_{2}$ oz black olives, pitted
6 tablespoons extra virgin olive oil
tiny basil leaves to garnish

Other Ideas

➤ A quick guacamole can be assembled in the liquidizer: avocados, shallot, chilli, lemon juice, olive oil and chopped tomato. Scoop it on to corn chips.

➤ The guacamole theme would translate well to a Thai hot and sour dressing made with a light soy sauce, caster sugar, lemon or lime juice and a little chopped chilli, with some sliced red onion and coriander leaves.

➤ When making a chilled avocado soup the trick is to make a soup base with stock and flavourings, such as lemon grass, or chopped shallot and a hint of garlic, then liquidize with the avocado flesh just before serving. This way it does not get time to discolour.

➤ Serve halved avocados filled with tomato salsa.

➤ Add avocado slices to young leeks in vinaigrette and scatter with slivers of black olive.

➤ Make a salad with asparagus, avocado, broad beans and toasted pine-nuts.

➤ Dress slices of avocado with a hazelnut vinaigrette, chopped and toasted hazelnuts, and a sprinkling of cayenne. Optional extra: a few drops of anise liqueur such as Ricard.

See also:

Artichoke Hearts Filled with Avocado Purée – Shallot Vinaigrette (page 3)
Chicory and Avocado Caesar Salad (page 68)
Gazpacho (page 192)

Beetroot

To herald a vegetable on account of its colour is enough to strike the fear of nouvelle cuisine into anyone. All those feathered purée assemblies in contrasting green, white and vermilion. And yet I am the first to marvel at a garnet-red risotto, with a creamy dollop of mascarpone melting over it. Or a purée of beetroot enriched with sour cream, surrounded with deep-fried parsley.

Risottos, purées and soups are ideal showplaces for beetroot to flaunt its glorious colour. The flip side of the coin being its tendency to bleed, which can be a problem – no one wants pink smears across their quail's eggs. With salads, the way round this is to make a separate beetroot relish or little salad, arrange the other ingredients on a dish and place the beetroot in the centre, or just scatter it over at the very end, rather than tossing it in.

The natural sweetness of beetroot makes it a candidate for marrying with other sweet ingredients. It makes a dramatic sweet and sour pickle, spiced with cinnamon sticks, cloves and coriander seeds. And you can make a beetroot cake, in classic carrot style. Sheila Lukins gives a recipe for a beetroot and rhubarb compote in her *All Around the World Cookbook* – 'one of the most unusual and delectable condiments I tasted on my journey through Scandinavia', excellent with roasted duck and pheasant, and with baked mackerel or salmon.

Beetroot marries well with fruit – not only with rhubarb but cooked in a sweet and sour fashion and garnished with red and white currants, raspberries, or combined with apples in a soup. Fruits accentuate its natural sweetness and provide much-needed acidity. Of other natural partners consider mushrooms, especially wild ones; and adding it to salads, with quail's eggs and green beans; salty blue cheeses; finely diced shallots; walnuts, hazelnuts and their associate oils; and chicory. Those slightly aniseedy herbs like tarragon, dill and chervil also suit it well; and you can flavour a purée with a hint of pastis.

In *Vegetable Magic* Guy Savoy suggests serving moules marinière with a julienne of beetroot that has been fried in butter. He also grills whiting fillets with a beetroot butter.

Gardeners can grow golden beetroots, which I have never come across in shops – even more exciting is 'Chioggia', an old Italian variety that sports concentric red and white rings.

Selection

Try to buy beetroots with their leaves attached – these should be green and fresh. Aim for medium-sized raw beetroot of the same size; if you have a mixture of sizes they are going to cook at different rates, and large ones tend to be fibrous.

Cooking

Ready-made vinegared beetroots are often soused with a second-rate vinegar and will overpower just about any salad you put them in. If I'm pushed for time I do buy the vac-pacs of cooked and peeled beetroot, but as a rule I cook them myself, because it's so easy and the flavour and freshness cannot be beaten.

A long slow roasting allows the sugars in beetroot to develop, and you will also get a more developed taste of the beetroot itself. Boiling it risks those precious pink juices leaching into the cooking water, and as the skin becomes quite fragile during the process this is always a risk.

Preheat the oven to 160°C fan oven/170°C or 325°F electric oven/Gas 3. If the beetroots are very dirty then scrub them, but most supermarket beetroots do not require this. Leave any whiskery roots and stems intact. Place them in a baking dish, cover loosely with foil and cook for 2 hours, or longer if they are large. The skin will wrinkle and separate from the flesh, and once they are cool enough to handle it should slip off with ease. If necessary, use a small paring knife to assist in peeling them.

Ricotta and Nutmeg Gnocchi with Beetroot Sauce

Potato gnocchi in beetroot sauce were a one-time speciality at the Italian restaurant Santini in Ebury Street, where they would serve a small pile along with a variety of pastas.

To make the sauce, cook and peel the beetroot as on page 25 and dice it. Heat the olive oil in a small saucepan and sweat the onion, beetroot and herbs for a few minutes until the onion is translucent. Add the cream and water, season with plenty of salt and pepper, bring back to the boil and simmer for 3 minutes. Remove the herbs and liquidize the sauce, sharpening it with a few drops of lemon juice. This sauce can be reheated.

Combine the flour, seasoning and nutmeg in a bowl. Blend the ricotta and egg yolks in another bowl. Add the flour to the ricotta mixture and work until it is just blended but do not overmix: the mixture will be sticky.

Flour a work surface. Take about a fifth of the mixture at a time and roll it by hand into a long, thin sausage 1 cm/½ inch in diameter. Cut this into slices 0.5 cm/¼ inch thick. Press the tines of a fork on one of the cut sides of each slice, flattening it. Lay a tea-towel on a tray, sprinkle it with flour, and reserve the gnocchi in a single layer, covered with another tea-towel. Do this as close to the time of serving as possible, though you can keep them in a cool place for a short while.

To cook the gnocchi, bring a large pan of salted water to the boil. Add the gnocchi; they will rise to the surface after a minute or two. Give them one minute longer, then strain and toss with the hot sauce. Serve with a dollop of mascarpone in the centre and a few chives scattered over.

Photograph opposite page 33.

Serves 4

Sauce
225 g/8 oz uncooked medium-sized beetroot (150 g/5½ oz when cooked and peeled)
1 tablespoon extra virgin olive oil
½ onion, peeled and chopped
1 small sprig of rosemary
1 small sprig of sage
125 ml/4 fl oz double cream
125 ml/4 fl oz water
sea salt and freshly ground black pepper
a few drops of lemon juice

Gnocchi
150 g/5½ oz plain flour, or Farina 00 (a flour used for making pasta; it can be found in Italian delis), sifted
sea salt and freshly ground black pepper
½ teaspoon freshly grated nutmeg
450 g/1 lb ricotta
2 medium egg yolks

To serve
mascarpone
finely chopped chives

Beetroot, French Bean and Hazelnut Salad with Toasted Goat's Cheese

For this you need the small individual demi-sec goat's cheeses such as the Innes buttons, or Crottins de Chavignol.

Heat the oven to 160°C fan oven/170°C or 335°F electric oven/ Gas 3. Scrub the beetroots if they are very dirty. Place them in a shallow baking dish and bake for 1–2 hours or until a knife can be inserted with ease. Allow to cool to room temperature.

While the beetroot is cooking, whisk the vinegar with the seasoning and add the oils. Separate a third of the dressing and whisk in the mustard; add the dill to the remaining dressing.

Bring a large pan of salted water to the boil. Top and tail the beans and add them to the pan, then bring back to the boil and cook for 3–4 minutes. Drain the beans and cool in a sink of cold water. Remove to a bowl and toss with the mustard dressing.

Remove the beetroot skins – these should be wrinkled and come away quite easily, but use a knife as necessary. Cut the flesh into 0.75 cm/ ⅓ inch dice and place in a bowl. Toss with the dill dressing and stir in the hazelnuts.

To serve the salad, preheat the grill, place the goat's cheese on a baking dish and grill until it is patched with brown (a demi-sec cheese will hold its shape). Place the beans on the base of 4 plates or one large one and place the beetroot in a pile in the centre, with the goat's cheese to one side.

Serves 4

700 g/1 lb 9 oz medium-sized uncooked beetroot (400 g/14 oz when cooked and peeled)
1 tablespoon red wine vinegar
sea salt and freshly ground black pepper
4 tablespoons hazelnut oil
3 tablespoons groundnut oil
1 level teaspoon grainy mustard
1 heaped tablespoon finely chopped dill
350 g/12 oz fine French beans
20 g/¾ oz roasted and chopped hazelnuts
175 g/6 oz demi-sec goat's cheese

Beetroot Tzatziki

This is a louche shade of pink and sweeter than the traditional tzatziki. It would go nicely with smoked fish such as eel or salmon, or you could serve it as part of a selection of mezze dishes. I have also eaten it with barbecued chicken, a bowl of watercress and a potato salad, which made a delicious combination.

Whisk the olive oil, vinegar and yoghurt together in a bowl and season with salt. Peel the cucumber, quarter lengthwise, remove the seeds, and finely dice the flesh by first slicing the quarters into thin strips. Peel the cooked beetroot and finely dice this too. Add the cucumber, beetroot, shallot and herbs to the tzatziki, cover and chill until required. To serve, first stir it well, then decorate with a swirl of olive oil and a sprinkling of chopped dill.

Serves 4

1 tablespoon extra virgin olive oil
1 teaspoon white wine vinegar
225 g/8 oz Greek yoghurt
sea salt
10 cm/4 inch piece of cucumber
175 g/6 oz cooked beetroot
1 heaped teaspoon finely chopped shallot
1 heaped teaspoon finely chopped dill
½ teaspoon finely chopped mint

To serve
extra virgin olive oil
finely chopped dill

Other Ideas

➤ Make a classic salad of blanched French beans, Roquefort, walnuts, beetroot and chives, and dress with red wine vinegar and walnut oil.

➤ Grate beetroot and cook in butter until tender, then blend it with ricotta cheese and chopped dill and use it as a stuffing for little patties made with thinly rolled puff or shortcrust pastry, then baked.

➤ Serve a chilled beetroot soup with two coloured creams drizzled over: a white and a green – for instance, parsley blanched and liquidized with cream, and some cooked celeriac also liquidized with cream.

➤ Dress hot butter beans with extra virgin olive oil, season and add some chopped shallot. Serve hot, with diced beetroot mixed with a little butter and lemon juice on top.

➤ Assemble an old-fashioned platter of hors d'oeuvres: separate piles of pickled herrings, green beans and cashew nuts mixed, a potato salad with mayonnaise, boiled quail's eggs, and a beetroot salad.

➤ Serve beetroot caviar with pancakes, lots of melted butter, crème fraîche and chives, and smoked salmon.

➤ Make a chunky club sandwich with rye bread, Dolcelatte, lots of watercress, macadamia nuts and sweet and sour beetroot.

➤ Do as Edouard de Pomiane does in his *Cooking in 10 Minutes*: Minced Beetroot à la Crème – 'Peel and wash half a pound of beetroot cooked in the oven. Dry it. Chop it finely. Heat some butter in a frying pan until it smokes. Warm the beetroot in it. Salt. Add a teaspoonful of vinegar. The beetroot immediately turns to a flaming hue. Add two ounces of thick cream. Mix. Warm for two minutes. Arrange it in a small dish. Cover it with a blanket of thick cream. Serve as hors d'oeuvre.'

Broad Beans

The first batch of fresh broad beans each year is a real treat – that pleasure of splitting open the pods and running your thumb along the downy inside to extract the beans. Sadly there are never many beans to show for all those pods, and if I am brutally honest I had best admit that I often turn to frozen broad beans. I use very little in the way of frozen food, but broad beans are not to be sniffed at as being inferior; they are of an extremely high quality and, unlike frozen peas, which are lovely but which bear little resemblance to their fresh equivalent, frozen broad beans are not that dissimilar from fresh ones.

I am also fond of dried broad beans, which you can find in Middle Eastern delis. These are delicious cooked for several hours until they turn into a purée, eaten with a slick covering of olive oil and some grated Parmesan.

But it is gardeners who can fully exploit this vegetable: a favourite delicacy of mine is broad bean tops wilted in butter, exquisitely sweet and tender. The pods too can be eaten while they are young. Nada Saleh, author of *Fragrance of the Earth*, a book on Lebanese cookery, makes the most delicious dish of broad beans in oil – whole pods are braised with onions until they are tender, and the stew is flavoured with cinnamon, allspice and lots of lemon juice and coriander. Later in the year when the pods have become fibrous I make this dish with runner beans.

Now and again when time is tight I rope my husband into helping with recipes, and he is always extremely obliging – except, that is, when it comes to skinning broad beans. There is no pretending that this task, which leaves your hands puckered and stained, is especially pleasant. Some cooks I know feel it is a nonsense, and if the broad beans are small then certainly it is unnecessary, but as they become large, which happens surprisingly early on in the season, the skins really do get quite tough and towards the end of the season the inner bean becomes mealy. Also, in shops broad beans do tend to be sold large rather than small.

If you are going to skin them it helps if only a few ounces are called for in a recipe. If using fresh then skin them after cooking; if frozen, thaw and then skin. If you are making a purée or a soup, you can get around it by puréeing the beans, skins and all, and passing the purée through a sieve.

Three Bean Salad Served Warm with Balsamic Vinaigrette

Three bean salad was one of the clichés that dragged the name of vegetarian cookery down to its stodgy depths, existing as a selection of tinned kidney beans and tinned sweetcorn with a few flabby French beans thrown in. None of that here, I promise: this is a mélange of tender butter beans, broad beans and French beans tossed while warm with a balsamic vinaigrette and chopped shallots.

If you need an instant salad there is no reason why you should not use tinned butter beans or haricots; you will need about 250 g/9 oz of drained beans.

Preheat the oven to 170°C fan oven/180°C or 350°F electric oven/ Gas 4. Rinse and drain the butter beans, put them in a flameproof casserole and cover them with 5 cm/2 inches of water. No salt should be added until the beans are cooked, otherwise it will toughen the skins. Bring the beans to the boil on top of the stove and skim any surface foam. Cover the casserole and place it in the centre of the oven for 45–60 minutes until the beans are tender. To avoid the skins cracking, leave the beans in the water until you need to toss them.

While the butter beans are cooking, top and tail the French beans and halve them. If the broad beans are very large, first thaw them with boiling water then skin them. To make the dressing, whisk the vinegar and lemon juice with the mustard and seasoning, then add the oil and shallots.

Bring a large pan of salted water to the boil. Add the French beans and the broad beans and boil for 4 minutes. Drain all the beans and toss with the dressing. Serve the salad warm, or when it has cooled down.

Photograph between pages 56 and 57.

Serves 4

115 g/4 oz butter beans, soaked overnight
175 g/6 oz French beans
250 g/9 oz frozen broad beans

Vinaigrette
1 tablespoon balsamic vinegar
1 tablespoon lemon juice
¾ teaspoon Dijon mustard
sea salt and freshly ground black pepper
6 tablespoons extra virgin olive oil
25 g/1 oz finely chopped shallot (approx. 2)

Broad Bean and Thyme Risotto

The essence of this risotto is the spoon of thyme cream that melts over the top. Occasionally thyme leaves can be woody, and ideally here they should be nice and tender. I have the luxury of lemon thyme, possibly my favourite herb, growing on the terrace; but if you grow summer savory, this too could be added to the cream, and you can also use chives. If you have any cooked asparagus tips lying around, these could be added at the end, with the broad beans.

Bring a large pan of water to the boil and cook the broad beans. The time this takes will depend on whether they are fresh or frozen – allow about 6 minutes for fresh. Cool the beans under running water, then skin and reserve them. Heat the stock to simmering point on the stove and keep it on a low heat while cooking the risotto.

Heat 50 g/1¾ oz of the butter in a heavy-bottomed pan and sweat the onion over a low heat until it is translucent and soft; it must not colour. Add the rice and cook for 1–2 minutes. Pour in the wine and continue to cook until it has been absorbed. Add the thyme sprigs and start to pour in ladles of simmering stock – at no stage should the rice be flooded. It will take about 25 minutes to cook; stop while the risotto is on the moist side.

To finish the risotto, stir in the Parmesan and the remaining butter. Remove the thyme sprigs and add the broad beans to heat through. Adjust the seasoning and serve with a spoon of the thyme cream in the centre.

Serves 4

350 g/12 oz young broad beans
1 litre/1¾ pints light vegetable stock
85 g/3 oz unsalted butter
1 small onion, peeled and finely chopped
285 g/10 oz risotto rice, Arborio or
    Carnaroli
150 ml/5 fl oz white wine
6 sprigs of thyme
60 g/2 oz freshly grated Parmesan
sea salt and freshly ground black pepper

Thyme cream
2 heaped teaspoons chopped thyme
    with 3 heaped dessertspoons crème
    fraîche

Artichoke Hearts Filled with Avocado Purée – Shallot Vinaigrette (page 3)

Brioche Sandwich Filled with Aubergine Fritters, Saffron Mayonnaise and Chutney (page 16)

Avocado with Tabbouleh and Fried Haloumi (page 20)

Ten Minute Broad Bean Soup with Tapenade

A genuine quicky that takes advantage of frozen broad beans. A jar of shop-bought tapenade is extremely useful to have in the fridge. The best I have tasted I brought back with me from the South of France. Their quality does depend on the brand. In the absence of such convenience I have included a recipe for tapenade below; the excess should keep well in the fridge for at least a week.

Melt the butter in a medium-sized saucepan and sweat the onion and garlic until translucent and soft. Add the wine and reduce until the liquor is syrupy. Add the broad beans and the vegetable stock, bring to the boil and simmer for 5 minutes. Liquidize and pass through a sieve, add the cream and seasoning, and reheat.

Stir the tapenade into the crème fraîche and serve this spooned over the hot soup, in hot bowls, with lots of crusty bread.

Tapenade

Purée all the ingredients together in a food processor until you have a thick paste.

Serves 3

25 g/1 oz unsalted butter
1 white onion, peeled and chopped
1 garlic clove, peeled and finely chopped
150 ml/5 fl oz white wine
450 g/1 lb frozen broad beans
750 ml/1½ pints vegetable stock
150 ml/5 fl oz whipping cream
sea salt and freshly ground black pepper

Tapenade cream
1 teaspoon tapenade (recipe below)
2 tablespoons crème fraîche

Tapenade
125 g/4½ oz black olives, pitted
15 g/½ oz capers
pinch of thyme
1 teaspoon brandy (optional)
½ garlic clove
1 tablespoon extra virgin olive oil
freshly ground black pepper
1 tablespoon crème fraîche

Ricotta and Nutmeg Gnocchi with Beetroot Sauce (page 26)

Other Ideas

➤ Make a frittata with broad beans and strips of wilted red pepper, artichoke or courgette. For this you need about 450 g/1 lb cooked vegetables, mixed into 6 eggs beaten into 150 ml/¼ pint double cream with a little Parmesan: pour into a gratin dish and bake for 20 minutes in a hottish oven.

➤ Skin cooked broad beans and add to a potato salad dressed with a herb vinaigrette and chopped shallots.

➤ Make a risotto of young spring vegetables with broad beans included.

➤ Make a rice salad using half wild rice and half basmati; add broad beans, asparagus and dill.

➤ Turn older, tough broad beans into a purée enriched with olive oil, garlic, lemon juice, ground cumin and ground coriander. Serve with fresh coriander and with olive oil poured over, accompanied by pitta bread.

➤ Include broad beans in a chunky minestrone style of soup, with vegetables such as carrots, turnips, green beans, fennel and porcini mushrooms.

See also:

Gratin of Artichoke Hearts with Broad Beans (page 5)
Seven Vegetable Tagine (page 132)

Broccoli

Broccoli has curves like green hills rolling into the distance, but close up it is a mass of tiny buds. We know it in three different forms, the most common being calabrese, green and occasionally purple; and then there is the purple sprouting type, and the very beautiful romanesco, a head consisting of spiralled turrets – whenever I see this I wonder that nature has created anything quite so beautiful.

Although nine times out of ten broccoli appears as a side vegetable, either steamed or boiled, this does not do justice to its potential – especially when dressed with sharp oriental dressings with sesame oil and seeds for serving with seared tuna, teriyaki and so forth. It also suits the Sicilian treatment of cauliflower – braised with olives, chilli, garlic, Pecorino (or Caciocavallo) and red wine – even though it is not quite as robust in texture.

Although it is the florets for which we buy it, don't discard the trimmings; once deflowered, broccoli may have the semblance of a sawn-off tree trunk which even the least cosmetically aware would not choose to dish up, but these parts are superb for soups and purées, and the greens that surround the purple sprouting buds can be cooked as a vegetable. Alternatively the stalks can be peeled and sliced, then cooked along with the flowering heads.

Purple sprouting broccoli is so rare it appears on menus bathed in Hollywood lights during its brief growing season. Purple sprouting has a distinct bitterness and, failing to find it once upon a time, I took a tip from the chef at Alastair Little Lancaster Road: to achieve that requisite bitterness you can combine the ordinary broccoli with a small amount of spring greens or radicchio.

Selection

Always buy broccoli that is compact; there should be no yellowing buds. It does deteriorate quite quickly, so it is best to store it in the bottom of the fridge.

Cooking

The flowering part is likely to cook faster than any thick stalks; these can be removed and cut into batons, or peeled and sliced as mentioned above.

Either steam it or cook it in boiling salted water – a few minutes should do. If I am using it for a salad I cool it immediately in cold water to preserve the colour and arrest the cooking, but this does detract a little from the flavour.

Small florets can be sautéed as they are, but if there are thick stalks it will need steaming. 'Smothering' is one of my preferred treatments: first sauté it in olive oil with garlic and finely chopped chilli, maybe with some anchovies, then add a splash of water, stock or wine, cover the pan and cook for a couple of minutes longer.

Lebanese Pancakes Filled with Broccoli and Mozzarella

These pancakes are unlike any others I have encountered, cooked on just one side and then stuffed – souffléd, in effect. I have adapted the recipe from one in *Fragrance of the Earth* by Nada Saleh.

To prepare the pancakes, first dissolve the yeast in 3 teaspoons of water in a small bowl, add the sugar and salt and leave until the surface froths. Sieve the flour and baking powder into a bowl. Gradually add 350 ml/12 fl oz hand-hot water and whisk until smooth, then add the yeast mixture. Cover and leave in a warm place for 2 hours.

To prepare the filling, finely slice the broccoli and place in a sauté pan with the olive oil, 4 tablespoons of water, a squeeze of lemon juice and the seasoning. Cover and cook for 10 minutes until very tender. Once cool, drain off any excess juices and mix with the mozzarella.

To cook the pancakes, heat the oil in a frying pan over a medium heat, tipping out the excess when it is hot. Spoon 2 tablespoons of the batter into the frying pan and spread it to a diameter of 15 cm/6 inches, using the spoon – these are thick pancakes almost like blinis. Once the top side appears pitted and dry, remove it from the pan. Cook the remaining pancakes in the same fashion, if necessary adding a little more oil to the pan.

Stuff the pancakes as they are cooked: place a tablespoon of filling on one half and fold the pancake into a half moon, pressing the edges together firmly to seal them.

Preheat the oven to 200°C fan oven/220°C or 425°F electric oven/ Gas 7. Brush both sides of the pancakes with the melted butter and lay them on a baking tray. Cook for 10 minutes – they should be nicely crisp on the outside. Serve with sprigs of watercress.

Makes 10, serves 4

Pancakes
1½ teaspoons dried yeast
½ teaspoon caster sugar
pinch of sea salt
200 g/7 oz plain flour
1 heaped teaspoon baking powder
1 tablespoon groundnut or vegetable oil

Filling
200 g/7 oz broccoli
1 tablespoon olive oil
squeeze of lemon juice
sea salt and freshly ground black pepper
2 buffalo mozzarellas, chopped
40 g/1½ oz unsalted butter, melted

To serve
watercress sprigs

Oriental Stir-fried Broccoli and Cauliflower

This always looks pretty, with its two-tone green and white, flecked with pale, toasted almonds. It goes extremely well with roast duck and chicken. You can expand it into a more substantial vegetarian dish with sautéed oyster or wild mushrooms and baby corn.

Bring a large pan of salted water to the boil. Divide the cauliflower up into florets, and also the broccoli: blanch the cauliflower for 2 minutes, and the broccoli for 1 minute. Drain and allow surface steam to evaporate.

Heat the olive oil in a large frying pan over a medium high heat. Add the ginger, garlic and chilli, and moments later the cauliflower and broccoli. Stir-fry for a few minutes, adding seasoning. Mix in the almonds. A few drops of soy sauce are optional.

Serves 3–4

1 cauliflower
350 g/12 oz broccoli (1 large head)
3 tablespoons extra virgin olive oil
1 heaped teaspoon finely chopped fresh
   ginger
1 heaped teaspoon finely chopped garlic
   (approx. 2 cloves)
1 level teaspoon finely chopped red chilli
sea salt and freshly ground black pepper
40 g/1½ oz toasted almond flakes

To serve
light soy sauce (optional)

Escabeche with Thyme Toast

These vegetables are lightly pickled, and quite hot with chilli. I have customized a recipe I found in the excellent American food magazine *Saveur*. This makes quite a substantial salad served with toasted pitta bread sprinkled with zaatar, a Middle Eastern mix of dried thyme, sesame seeds, sumac and sea salt. Sumac is a brick-red powder; the dried and ground berries of the sumac bush. It's very tart, and replaces lemon juice in some regions.

I was first given some zaatar by a Lebanese friend, who explained that the homemade version uses only the tips of the thyme, whereas the commercial ones available from Middle Eastern delis use the entire plant. Ever since first acquiring some, I have found that a small jar of zaatar in the cupboard and some pitta bread (which can be kept in the freezer) is the answer to all manner of soups, snacks and salads. The pitta is first toasted in the oven, then slit; olive oil is drizzled over and it is scattered with the herbal mix. In the absence of zaatar use dried oregano, or thyme, and sea salt. As to the vegetables, gardeners can play around with yellow courgettes or pattypans, lemon thyme, young carrots and so forth.

Heat the olive oil in a large saucepan and sauté the garlic and onion over a medium heat for a few minutes, stirring. Add the carrots, peppercorns, thyme and bay leaves. Cover and cook for 1–2 minutes — the onion should have a touch of colour without turning brown. Season with salt, then add the broccoli, chilli, vinegar and 125 ml/4 fl oz water. Bring to the boil, cover and simmer for 2 minutes. Add the courgettes, cover, and cook for another 3 minutes. The vegetables should be cooked but remain fairly crunchy. Cool to room temperature before serving. You can chill it, covered, until required, and it keeps well for several days: bring it back to room temperature before you eat it.

Photograph opposite page 56.

Serves 4

7 tablespoons extra virgin olive oil
6 garlic cloves, peeled
1 small onion, peeled and cut into wedges
250 g/9 oz carrots, peeled and sliced on the bias
½ teaspoon whole black peppercorns
1 heaped teaspoon thyme
4 bay leaves
sea salt
250 g/9 oz broccoli florets (approx. 1 large head)
2 fresh red chillies, deseeded and chopped
175 g/6 fl oz white wine vinegar
400 g/14 oz yellow or green courgettes, sliced on the bias

Other Ideas

➤ Make a broccoli and almond soup by sweating chopped onion and finely sliced broccoli stalks along with the buds and some flaked almonds. Then add stock and simmer, liquidize, pass through a sieve and add some cream.

➤ Cook broccoli for about 1 hour with olive oil, a little water, whole garlic cloves and thyme until it reduces to a coarse purée.

➤ Sauté small broccoli florets in olive oil with a little chilli and garlic; add a splash of red wine vinegar, cook to reduce this, and serve scattered with crisp breadcrumbs.

➤ Sweat some red onions and thyme in olive oil until they are silky and well-cooked. Add some steamed broccoli florets and chopped black olives.

➤ Mash up well-cooked broccoli with ricotta cheese and grated Parmesan and use it to stuff ravioli, or filo pastries.

➤ Make a salad of cooked spring vegetables: broccoli florets, carrots, baby fennel, turnips, broad beans. Dress with a balsamic vinaigrette and scatter with snipped chives and chervil.

Cabbage

I only began to feel truly fond of cabbages after visiting a gardener whose love of them had given rise to the most stunning display of different varieties in his vegetable patch; like huge blowsy roses they dominated the garden. Consider beyond that how easily they are grown and how well they keep during the cold months, and it is easy to appreciate why we have such a tradition of cabbage cookery.

Cabbages are guilty as sin of being unpalatable if plainly boiled, but after experimenting with them I became quite a convert: there are ways of cooking them that release wonderful nutty and sweet aromas, which set your mind dancing around spices like juniper berries and nutmeg, tart fruits and balsamic vinegar, which bring them alive.

Cabbage seems to be getting a new lease of life, in part thanks to the Pacific Rim and the many 'choys' now available – although these are a separate entity from our own home-grown varieties. Still, there is an overlap: green, white and Savoy cabbage lends itself to sweet, sour and hot Thai dressings, and to being sautéed with a little sesame oil and soy sauce. Treated in this fashion, cabbage goes surprisingly well with fish, especially mackerel and grey mullet.

I have never come around to coleslaw, however. I have tried hard to give it a reprieve, concocting luscious mayonnaises and sweet and salty oriental dressings, but you never get rid of the 'cabbagey' flavour of eating it raw. The closest raw cabbage gets to palatability is when it is salted and then fermented, when it takes on a relaxed texture. The notion of fermenting a vegetable holds a certain fascination – sauerkraut is the most famed of this genre. It takes weeks, and is not something you are advised to try at home: a garage or outside shed is pretty much essential. Nor is it child's play: the temperature and humidity have to be just right, in between 15 and 21°C, otherwise it can turn, and initially it has to be skimmed. I won't go into lengthy details as I cannot see many of you making it at home.

More useful, I feel, is the lightly fermented version I ate at Alastair Little in Frith Street. Prepared by the chef, Juliet Preston, the cabbage was sweet, sour and spiced, served with turbot fried in a maize crust. This was related to kimchi, a Korean equivalent of sauerkraut; whereby 'Peking' or 'Napa' cabbage is salted, then buried in the earth and fermented. The Koreans dig into it throughout the year and it is hot with chillies and garlic.

You can make this sweet and sour cabbage overnight: first salt and weight shredded cabbage, using a plate. By leaving it out of the fridge you achieve the necessary hint of sourness – leave it for up to 4 days, then rinse it and mix in some thin strips of carrot and daikon radish. Preston makes a dressing with rice wine vinegar, saki, sugar, coriander, cumin, turmeric, chillies and grated ginger, and pickles the salted cabbage for several hours in a tray. It is an inspired interpretation.

In truth, though, my heart lies with all those jazzed up granny-style cabbage dishes. Sweet and sour red cabbage with plenty of brown sugar and vinegar, and either some apple or cranberries, or raisins and hazelnuts added, really creamy cabbage dishes with the faintest hint of caraway, or that great Irish colcannon, a blend of mashed potato and cabbage.

It is always worth cooking extra cabbage, in anticipation of opening the fridge and finding that you just happen to have a bowl of leftover mashed or boiled potatoes and a bowl of cooked cabbage which you can turn into bubble and squeak. Fry them together in butter or olive oil, a little garlic if you like, turning the cake each time the underside becomes golden and crispy, hence folding the crisp bits back into the cake. A bottle of Lea and Perrins on the table and you're away.

Preparation

Close-headed cabbages can be divided into red varieties, the Savoy cabbages with their blueish, crinkled leaves; green cabbages, which include 'January Kings', and the tightly closed white cabbages usually used for coleslaw.

All these cabbages keep well: peel away the outer leaves, and then, if you are slicing them, quarter and cut out the tough inner core and finely slice the quarters. I confess I do not subsequently wash the shredded cabbage. If you are removing leaves to stuff, prise off the outer 6–8 leaves, starting at the base end. You can then quarter and slice the hearts as normal. I have not included any recipes for individually stuffing leaves, something I feel is best left for restaurants. Instead I have given a recipe for a charlotte where the outside of the bowl is lined with leaves.

Loose-headed cabbages such as spring greens, and the Chinese varieties, require a different treatment to the close-headed types and are not included in this section.

Stuffed Cabbage with Porcini and Gruyère

Usually stuffed cabbage dishes alarm me on account of being fiddly, but then a friend suggested this method of cooking the outside leaves of a cabbage, lining a deep bowl, and layering the hearts with other ingredients inside. You turn it out and cut into it like a cake.

Cover the porcini with 150 ml/5 fl oz of boiling water and leave to soak for 15 minutes.

Bring a large pan of salted water to the boil. Discard any damaged outer leaves of the cabbage, then remove the outer 8 leaves and cut out the tough midribs. Quarter the remaining heart, cut out the hard core and slice the leaves.

Add the whole leaves to the pan, bring back to the boil, and cook for 4 minutes. Remove the leaves to a sink of cold water, then squeeze out thoroughly with your hands. Add the remaining cabbage to the pan, bring back to the boil, cook for 5 minutes and drain into a colander. Once cool, squeeze out with your hands.

Drain the porcini and chop them, reserving the liquor. Melt the butter in a frying pan and sweat the garlic and shallots for a couple of minutes. Add the chopped porcini to heat through, then the wine, and reduce by two-thirds. Add the cream and cook until it thickens, then add the reserved mushroom liquor, cook for a few minutes and season. Stir in the *beurre manié* and allow the sauce to thicken.

Butter an 18 cm/7 inch soufflé dish or equivalent mould. Reserving 1 leaf for the top, arrange the whole cabbage leaves on the base and around the sides, draping them over it. Now layer the sliced cabbage with the mushroom sauce and cheese, starting with a layer of cabbage. You will need three layers of cabbage and two of sauce and cheese: season the cabbage layers. Lay the reserved cabbage leaf on the top and enclose with the overhanging leaves. Cover with foil.

Preheat the oven to 190°C fan oven/200°C or 400°F electric oven/ Gas 6 and bake for 45 minutes. Invert on to a plate.

Serves 4

---

15 g/½ oz dried porcini
1 medium green cabbage (1.2 kg/ 2 lb 10 oz)
25 g/1 oz unsalted butter, and extra for the dish
1 garlic clove, peeled and finely chopped
2 shallots, peeled and finely chopped
150 ml/5 fl oz white wine
150 ml/5 fl oz double cream
sea salt and freshly ground black pepper
1 heaped teaspoon of *beurre manié* (an equal quantity of plain flour and unsalted butter, blended)
175 g/6 oz grated Gruyère

Stir-fried White Cabbage

Remove the outer leaves from the cabbage, quarter, discarding the core, and finely slice the leaves. Cook in 2 batches: heat the olive oil in a frying pan, add the garlic, and moments later add the cabbage and cook, tossing, until it is coloured at the edges like fried onions, and tender. Season while cooking with salt, pepper and nutmeg.

Serves 4–6

1 small white cabbage (750 g/1 lb 10 oz)
3 tablespoons extra virgin olive oil
2 garlic cloves, peeled and finely chopped
sea salt and freshly ground black pepper
freshly grated nutmeg

Sweet and Sour Red Cabbage with Cranberries

Discard the outer leaves of the cabbage, quarter it, remove the hard core and finely slice the leaves. Clarify the butter: melt it in a large saucepan, skim off the surface foam, decant the crystal yellow liquid (the clarified butter) and discard the milk solids on the base.

Return the clarified butter to the saucepan and sweat the cabbage with the seasoning until it gives off a nutty aroma and is glossy and relaxed. Add the balsamic vinegar and the sugar and cook to evaporate it. Add the red wine and bay leaves, cover the pan, turn the heat down low and braise for 17 minutes, stirring half-way through.

Add the cranberries, cover the pan, and cook for another 10 minutes, stirring half-way through. Serve with a dollop of mascarpone.

Serves 4

1 small red cabbage (approx. 800 g/
   1 lb 12 oz)
60 g/2½ oz unsalted butter
sea salt and freshly ground black pepper
2 tablespoons balsamic vinegar
40 g/1½ oz brown sugar
3 tablespoons red wine
2 bay leaves
50 g/2 oz cranberries

To serve
mascarpone

Caldo Verde

This hearty Portuguese soup often includes garlic sausage. The Portuguese make it using a variety of cabbage called 'Galega', not unlike spring greens. I like really thick slabs of toast with it; it's also a showplace for a good olive oil.

Remove the outer leaves from the cabbage, quarter, discarding the core, and slice the leaves very finely into grass-like strands. Peel and cube the potatoes and place in a saucepan with the garlic, tomato and water. Bring to the boil and simmer for 15 minutes, then mash to a coarse purée. Add the soy sauces and seasoning.

To serve, add the cabbage, bring back to the boil and simmer for 5 minutes. Adjust the seasoning and serve in warm bowls with 1–2 tablespoons of olive oil drizzled over each serving, and a scattering of coriander.

Serves 4–6

400 g/14 oz Savoy cabbage (trimmed weight)
900 g/2 lb maincrop potatoes
3 garlic cloves, peeled and finely chopped
1 beefsteak tomato, peeled, seeded and diced
1.4 litres/2½ pints water
1 tablespoon light soy sauce
1 tablespoon dark soy sauce
sea salt and freshly ground black pepper

To serve
extra virgin olive oil
3 tablespoons coarsely chopped coriander

Other Ideas

➤ Sauté shredded white cabbage in butter, add a little double cream and crushed caraway seeds, and cook briefly until it thickens.

➤ Braise Savoy cabbage with butter, still cider and juniper berries.

➤ For sweet and sour red cabbage, cook shredded red cabbage with butter, balsamic vinegar and caster sugar until it is soft, and add roasted and chopped hazelnuts and raisins.

➤ Make bubble and squeak with cooked Savoy cabbage and boiled sweet potatoes: fry them in olive oil and butter until nice and crisp. Serve with soy sauce.

➤ Make a gratin by layering cooked white or Savoy cabbage with cooked and peeled chestnuts, cream, and a little white wine and vegetable stock, and bake until the surface is golden.

➤ Wrap cooked cabbage leaves around individual goat's cheeses, secure with a toothpick, drizzle with olive oil and roast in a hot oven for 15 minutes.

➤ Sauté shredded red cabbage with red onions and thyme.

Carrots

Carrot quality has mostly to do with size. The little winklings the size of your small finger might look great on a mosaic arrangement surrounding a piece of meat or fish, but they are pathetically endowed with flavour. The smallest that is acceptable is 'young', as opposed to 'baby'. I quite like seeing a mop of lacy green foliage attached – it is some guarantee of freshness, though having bought them you should remove the tops because they continue to extract the wherewithal to survive from the carrot itself, robbing it of nutrients.

As to types, I have never gone great guns over purple potatoes, such as the varieties 'Edgecote Purple', 'German Black' and 'Salad Blue', with their blue-tinged skins and creamy flesh streaked with purple, and I'm not sure I like the idea of purple carrots any better. Orange carrots will do me fine, and if there is to be any deviation then it is the squat little Parisian ones, which have an especially good flavour, that I would choose. Young carrots with their leaves attached are the ones I peel and keep in a bowl of water in the fridge for dunking into hummus and guacamole, or eating with a few slices of cheese throughout the day.

Wherever possible I buy organic carrots: due to the scare over organophosphorous chemicals contaminating their skins, it is possible to find these in supermarkets that do not otherwise bother with organic produce. Not only is their flavour superior – organic carrots don't break the bank in quite the same way as organic avocados.

Carrots are an essential element of a springtime mélange, be it steamed and served on top of a risotto along with broadbeans and peas, asparagus, and broccoli or cauliflower, or served in a light, creamy broth flavoured with lemon grass and scattered with chopped coriander.

The flavour of large carrots is good, but you do start to lose out on texture, so I usually turn these into soups or purées. Carrots marry especially well with spices – the first-century Roman author Apicius cooked and served them with olive oil and cumin, which seems remarkably modern. A carrot soup can be flavoured with a hint of curry powder (it will make all the difference if it is freshly ground); buttery purées, too, appreciate a grating of nutmeg or a pinch of cinnamon. And then of course there are spicy carrot cakes.

Michel Guérard's Carrot Flan – Jerusalem Artichoke Purée

I have rather shamelessly upped those rich ingredients Guérard sought to exclude: the flan recipe comes from *Cuisine Minceur*. The purée is not essential and you could use some other vegetable for it.

You can cook the purée in advance, or while the carrot flan is in the oven. Bring a large pan of water to the boil and acidulate it with a slug of vinegar. Peel the artichokes and cook them for 15 minutes until tender. Drain, place in a liquidizer, and purée with the crème fraîche, seasoning and lemon juice.

Melt the butter in a medium-sized saucepan and sweat the carrots until they begin to colour. Add the sugar, seasoning and wine, cover, and simmer over a low heat for 8 minutes. If any liquid remains cook with the lid off until it evaporates. Remove the carrots to a board and coarsely chop.

Heat the groundnut oil in the same saucepan and cook the mushrooms for a few minutes until soft; again, if they give out any liquid, cook until it evaporates.

Heat the oven to 190°C fan oven/200°C or 400°F electric oven/ Gas 6. Whisk the egg with the egg yolk, cream, Gruyère and parsley. Stir in the carrots and mushrooms and check the seasoning. Butter an 18 cm/7 inch soufflé dish or similar ovenproof mould, and line with a circle of buttered paper parchment. Spoon the mixture into the mould, cover with foil, and bake in a bain-marie for 30–45 minutes until the custard has set (a bain-marie is a water bath filled with boiling water, which should be about the same depth as the custard). Invert the flan on to a plate and serve in wedges with the hot purée.

Serves 4

Carrot flan
25 g/1 oz unsalted butter
700 g/1 lb 9 oz young carrots, peeled and thinly sliced
1 level teaspoon caster sugar
sea salt and freshly ground black pepper
100 ml/3½ fl oz white wine
1 dessertspoon groundnut oil
165 g/6 oz mushrooms, finely chopped
1 medium egg plus 1 egg yolk
100 ml/3 fl oz double cream
165 g/6 oz Gruyère, grated
2 heaped tablespoons coarsely chopped parsley

Jerusalem artichoke purée
white wine vinegar for acidulating water
700 g/1 lb 9 oz Jerusalem artichokes
2 heaped tablespoons crème fraîche
sea salt and freshly ground black pepper
squeeze of lemon juice

Provençal Hors d'Oeuvres

Tapenade and goat's cheese dip are especially good eaten in unison. Accompany with batons of carrot, cherry tomatoes, grissini bread sticks and radishes — the long ones are the most peppery. In my household the carrots seem to disappear before everything else, so have lots of these.

Green Olive Tapenade

Ideally use cracked green olives — I buy ones that have been marinated with spices and a little chilli. The waxy bottled offerings are not up to tapenade.

➤ Pit the olives and place in a food processor with the garlic, capers, basil and pepper. Process to a coarse paste. Add the olive oil and continue to whizz for a minute or two. Serve in a small bowl, garnished with a few fine slivers of spring onion.

Goat's Cheese Dip

➤ Remove the rind from the cheese and crumble into a bowl. Mash to a coarse paste with the olive oil and black pepper. Serve in a small bowl, garnished with a few fine slivers of spring onion.

Serves 6

Green Olive Tapenade

225 g/8 oz green olives
½ garlic clove
1 tablespoon capers, rinsed
1 tablespoon shredded basil
freshly ground black pepper
3 tablespoons extra virgin olive oil
a few slivers of spring onion, white and
    green parts

Goat's Cheese Dip

175 g/6 oz medium-mature goat's
    cheese, e.g. Crottin de Chavignol
3 tablespoons extra virgin olive oil
freshly ground black pepper
a few slivers of spring onion, white and
    green parts

Saffron-glazed Carrots

This is a side-dish in which the carrots are glazed with honey and flavoured with saffron. I like them nice and tender, so the cooking time renders them quite well done.

Peel the carrots and cut into batons about 5 cm/2 inches long (if they are small, leave them whole). Melt the butter in a medium-sized saucepan and sweat the carrots for a few minutes, then add the honey, saffron, herbs and seasoning and cook for a minute until they are well coated. Add the wine, cover and cook over a low heat for 10 minutes, stirring half-way through. The liquid should be absorbed.

Serves 4

650 g/1 lb 6 oz carrots
25 g/1 oz unsalted butter
1 teaspoon honey
15 saffron filaments (a pinch)
5 sprigs of thyme
2 bay leaves
sea salt and freshly ground black pepper
100 ml/3½ fl oz white wine

Oriental Late Summer Salad

I grow increasingly fond of oriental-style dressings for salads – there is virtually no oil involved here, so it is very light, but packed with flavour. All the vegetables should be on the young side, especially the runner beans.

Place all the ingredients for the poaching liquor in a medium-sized saucepan and bring to the boil. Cover, simmer for 5 minutes, strain and return to the pan.

Cut the carrots into thin batons about 5 cm/2 inches long, and the beans into similar lengths. Now poach the vegetables in the liquor, starting with the cauliflower. Do this in 2 lots: add to the simmering water, cover and cook for 3 minutes, then remove to a large serving plate with a slotted spoon. Cook the beans likewise for 3–4 minutes and the carrots for 2–3 minutes and add to the plate, reserving the liquor. Remove the seeds from the chilli, slice it and mix it with the vegetables.

Make a dressing with 4 tablespoons of the reserved cooking liquor – if it has reduced to less than this, make it up with water. Dissolve the sugar, add the soy sauce and sesame oil, and pour this dressing over the salad. Leave to cool to room temperature, about 10 minutes, then remove the chilli. Mix in the sesame seeds just before serving.

Serves 4

Poaching liquor
600 ml/1 pint vegetable stock
2 shallots, peeled and finely chopped
1 teaspoon finely chopped fresh ginger
1 teaspoon finely chopped lemon grass
2 sprigs of thyme
juice of ½ lemon
1 teaspoon sea salt

Salad
250 g/9 oz carrots, trimmed and peeled
250 g/9 oz runner beans, top and tailed
500 g/1 lb 2 oz small cauliflower florets
½ red chilli
½ teaspoon caster sugar
2 tablespoons light soy sauce
1 tablespoon sesame oil
1 heaped tablespoon sesame seeds, toasted in a dry frying pan

Other Ideas

- Dress grated young carrots with a mustardy vinaigrette made with red wine vinegar and olive oil – add either chopped and roasted hazelnuts or chopped parsley.

- Sweat thinly sliced carrots in butter until they are tender; add double cream and cook until it reduces to a thick coating sauce, then season and stir in lots of chopped chervil.

- Stir-fry a selection of carrots, cauliflower, beanshoots, aubergine and peas in groundnut and sesame oil: add young spinach leaves at the end, a sprinkling of sesame seeds and a shake of soy sauce.

- Enrich carrot purées and soups with mascarpone or crème fraîche.

- Enhance the sweetness of carrots by glazing them: cook them with a small amount of water, butter, honey or a pinch of sugar and seasoning until they are tender and there is no water left.

- To make a gratin of young carrots, first cook them and then lay them in a shallow dish and cover with a savoury custard of cream, egg yolks and a small amount of beaten whole egg, with grated Gruyère on top. Bake until the surface is golden.

See also:

Escabeche with Thyme Toast (page 38)
Roasted Root Vegetables with Rocket Pesto (page 130)
Seven Vegetable Tagine (page 132)

Cauliflower

'Cauliflower is nothing but a cabbage with a college education,' said Mark Twain. It is one of the more elegant members of the cabbage family; a flower vegetable that consists of a mass of tiny ivory buds that together form a textured curd (*caulis* is the Latin for 'stalk', and *floris* for 'of the flower').

Even though we usually find cauliflower in its white form, there is a lot of variety within this brassica. It comes in shades of the palest green through to the winegum-red Purple Cape Broccoli, which bears more similarity to a cauliflower than to broccoli but it is referred to under either banner. In Sicily they make quite an ado about the green varieties, known there as *broccolo*, just to confuse matters. I recall being stunned by displays of these green cauliflowers, stacked into pyramids many feet in height, when I walked around the market in Palermo. According to John Evelyn, writing in the seventeenth century, the finest cauliflowers came from Denmark and Russia. However, there does not seem to be any lengthy tradition of Russian cauliflower dishes other than pickles, which are not dissimilar to the Escabeche on page 38.

Ask any Brit to name the most famous cauliflower dish and the answer will be cauliflower cheese. It is also likely to be their least favourite. Having attended a boarding school where they specialized in gruesome gratins – a whole range of them – I can sympathize with this, but it has not put me off and I still adore cauliflower cheese. The spoilt child's version, that is, where a velouté is flavoured with masses of herbs and the cauliflower layered with raclette which melts to a divinely creamy river (recipe below).

The Sicilians can also teach us a thing or two about cooking cauliflowers. In one of my favourite dishes they are layered with Pecorino (Caciocavallo if you are in Sicily), black olives, anchovies and red wine and sweated until they are tender and deliciously gamey in flavour.

Cauliflower goes well in pasta dishes, using a squat tubular pasta, with toasted pine-nuts, currants and saffron. Or it can be mashed down with other ingredients to fill an empanada – a Spanish-style bread pie. But I have never taken to eating it raw.

Selection

Cauliflower should be really firm and a creamy ivory in colour; once it appears spongy and looks dull it is past its best. It is a good keeper – you can separate it into florets, wrap them in a plastic bag and store them in the bottom of the fridge for several days.

Cooking

Cauliflower is one of the easiest vegetables to prepare; it doesn't trap dirt and bugs and doesn't need peeling. Nor does it require lengthy cooking: it can be steamed, boiled or poached in a small amount of aromatic liquor for just a few minutes. I rather like cooking a cauliflower whole, pouring a sauce over it, and scattering over some crisply fried breadcrumbs. Cook it with about 1 cm/½ inch of water in the base of a covered pan, effectively steaming it. It will need a longer cooking time than florets, and a knife should insert with some ease into the thickest part of the base.

If I am going to sauté or stir-fry cauliflower I usually parboil it for a couple of minutes first, but if the florets are cut very small this isn't necessary. I rarely go to the trouble of adding lemon juice to the water to bleach cauliflower, because it's not as though it discolours in the dramatic fashion of artichokes, but you can do so if you like.

Gratin of Cauliflower with Crème Fraîche, Capers and Lemon

A break from cauliflower cheese — here it sits in a creamy sauce flavoured with capers and lemon, with crisp crumbs scattered over the top.

Preheat the oven to 200°C fan oven/220°C or 425°F electric oven/ Gas 7.

Bring a large pan of salted water to the boil. Add the cauliflower, bring back to the boil, cook for 2 minutes, then drain. Trim the base of the chicory heads and cut them into long thin strips. Melt 25 g/1 oz of the butter in a frying pan and cook the strips for a few minutes until soft and translucent.

Arrange the cauliflower and chicory in a shallow ovenproof dish and season. Blend the crème fraîche, cream, capers, lemon zest, juice and seasoning and pour over the vegetables. Bake for 20 minutes until colouring on top.

Meanwhile heat the remaining butter in the frying pan and cook the breadcrumbs with the garlic until they are crisp. Remove to a bowl and stir in the parsley. Scatter the crumbs over the cooked gratin, drizzle over the olive oil and return to the oven for 10 minutes.

Serves 4

750 g/1 lb 10 oz cauliflower florets (approx. 2 cauliflowers)
3 heads Belgian chicory
40 g/1½ oz unsalted butter
sea salt and freshly ground black pepper
150 ml/5 fl oz crème fraîche
150 ml/5 fl oz whipping cream
2 tablespoons capers, rinsed and chopped
finely grated zest of 1 lemon
squeeze of lemon juice
40 g/1½ oz breadcrumbs
1 garlic clove, peeled and finely chopped
2 tablespoons finely chopped flat-leaved parsley
1 tablespoon extra virgin olive oil

Cauliflower with a Herb Sauce and Raclette

A reprieve for cauliflower cheese.

To make the sauce, reduce the wine to one third of its volume in a small saucepan and combine it in a jug with the milk, cream and stock. Melt the butter in the same pan, add the flour, and cook the roux for 1–2 minutes. Gradually incorporate the liquid off the heat, whisking to disperse any lumps. Return to the heat and simmer for 5 minutes, stirring. Season with salt, pepper and nutmeg and stir in the mustard and herbs.

Heat the oven to 190°C fan oven/200°C or 400°F electric oven/ Gas 6. Bring a large pan of salted water to the boil, add the cauliflower, bring to the boil and cook for 5 minutes. Drain the cauliflower and arrange with the sauce and raclette in a shallow baking dish. Cover with foil and cook for 30–35 minutes until hot and bubbling at the edges. Serve with the croûtons scattered over.

Serves 4

650 g/1 lb 6 oz cauliflower florets
225 g/8 oz raclette (weight excluding rind),
  sliced

Sauce
150 ml/5 fl oz white wine
150 ml/5 fl oz milk
175 ml/6 fl oz double cream
175 ml/6 fl oz double strength vegetable
  stock
60 g/2 oz unsalted butter
40 g/1½ oz plain flour
sea salt, freshly ground black pepper and
  nutmeg
1 heaped teaspoon grainy mustard
1 heaped tablespoon each of finely chopped
  chives, chervil and flat-leaved parsley

To serve
diced croûtons fried in butter or clarified
  butter

Cauliflower in Almond Sauce

Instead of dividing the cauliflower up into florets you could also remove the inner core and cook the cauliflower whole, though obviously this will take longer.

To make the sauce, place the milk, cream, onion and bay leaf in a small saucepan and bring to a simmer; remove from the heat and infuse for 15 minutes, then strain. Blend the ground almonds with a little of the infused liquor so you have a smooth paste, then incorporate this back into the sauce base and season. Simmer over a very low heat for 10 minutes, stirring occasionally. Add the *beurre manié* and cook for a minute until slightly thickened and glossy.

To toast the almonds (if not using ready-toasted ones), heat the oven to 180°C fan oven/190°C or 375°F electric oven/Gas 5, place the almonds in a single layer on a baking sheet, and cook them for 7–8 minutes until lightly golden.

Bring a large pan of salted water to the boil. Cut the cauliflower into florets and boil them for 5 minutes, while you reheat the sauce. Drain the cauliflower thoroughly, arrange it on a warm serving plate, pour over the sauce and scatter over the almonds.

Serves 3

300 ml/½ pint milk
150 ml/5 fl oz double cream
1 small onion, peeled and stuck with 5 cloves
1 bay leaf
2 heaped tablespoons ground almonds
sea salt and freshly ground black pepper
1 heaped teaspoon *beurre manié* (made by mashing together equal quantities of plain flour and unsalted butter)
25 g/1 oz flaked or ready-toasted almonds
1 cauliflower

Escabeche with Thyme Toast (page 38)

Red Pepper and Celeriac Charlotte (page 60)

Three Bean Salad Served Warm with Balsamic Vinaigrette (page 31)

Other Ideas

- Cauliflower makes excellent à la grècque material, poached in an aromatic liquor flavoured with saffron and other whole spices and herbs, and sharpened with lemon juice. Strips of roasted red peppers added at the end would be nice.

- Steam or boil cauliflower florets and smother them in brown butter. To make this, first clarify unsalted butter by melting it, skimming off the surface foam, and decanting the clear yellow liquid, discarding the milky residue in the base. Return the yellow liquid to a clean pan and cook over a low heat until it is evenly brown. Scatter some toasted flaked almonds over the dressed cauliflower.

- Cauliflower makes good fritters for serving with tartare sauce or ravigote.

- Sauté cauliflower and broccoli with ginger, garlic and chilli in sesame oil.

- Cauliflower is essential to any mélange of spring vegetables and to a vegetable pot-au-feu or casserole of mixed vegetables.

- Dress cooked florets with olive oil, lemon juice, toasted and crushed spices like cumin and coriander, or chopped parsley, coriander or chives.

- A cream of cauliflower soup is delicate in both flavour and appearance. Serve with a dollop of mascarpone flavoured with freshly grated nutmeg.

See also:

Oriental Stir-fried Broccoli and Cauliflower (page 37)
Oriental Late Summer Salad (page 51)
Seven Vegetable Tagine (page 132)

Chicory and Avocado Caesar Salad (page 68)

Celeriac

I am very much fonder of celeriac than I am of celery. This could in part be down to celeriac rémoulade, a posh coleslaw, where fine strips sit in a creamy homemade mayonnaise flavoured with mustard, a classic among French salads. Rémoulade has northern hemisphere appeal. I think it's one of the best bits of a plateful of winter hors d'oeuvres, that and the beetroot and potato salad, not to mention a few gherkins. I also like it served inside marmande or beefsteak tomatoes, with a parsley vinaigrette. I tend to use celery in a supporting role along with carrots and leeks or onions rather than as a vegetable in its own right, except for soup, or the young hearts, which can be nice braised.

Celeriac is a comparative newcomer to England, first recorded in the 1720s. It is not in fact a root, as it may appear to be, but the swollen lower stem. Varieties have names like 'Alabaster', 'Marble Ball' and 'Snow White', which gives some notion of the hard cream-coloured interior that lies beneath the gnarled brown exterior.

Celeriac is inclined to lend itself to meat rather than fish, and especially to game – roasted around a pheasant or partridge it cooks to a meltingly tender inside. Mashed alone or with some potato it is wonderful for soaking up gravy juices. It is quite at home with spices, as the recipe for spiced celeriac mash illustrates. But I do not feel it is a vegetable that can be sold on its texture; it has a fabulous flavour and is at its best in purées, mash, soups and so forth.

There is another member of the celery family called smallage, a leafy variety eaten stalks and leaves together, which I have not tried. But I am a big fan of lovage, a bush which grows to huge dimensions in the garden. A young sprig or two can be treated as you would thyme, to provide a subtle celery scent for braised vegetables and stews. A little, though, goes a long way.

Selection

I tend to avoid the more threatening-looking examples with hundreds of tiny roots and hairs, it only means more waste. Try to buy ones that are quite smooth.

Preparation

I find it easiest to cut up celeriac once I have sliced off the outer skin. A large kitchen knife will help, but sometimes when it's really tough going I find the only solution is to ask my husband to help. If there is any delay in cooking it, store it in water acidulated with lemon juice or white wine vinegar. Acidulate the boiling water also.

Curried Celeriac Gratin

Perfect with plain baked potatoes; it takes only 10 minutes to assemble, and 1 hour and 10 minutes to bake, so they'll both be ready at the same time.

When you use curry powder in this sort of quantity to flavour a sauce, it is not necessary to fry it as you normally would. Be sure it is fresh, and a good blend.

Preheat the oven to 200°C fan oven/220°C or 425°F electric oven/ Gas 7.

Cut the skin off the celeriac, quarter and thinly slice it, working quickly to avoid it discolouring. Arrange the slices in a gratin dish or casserole, seasoning them. Whisk the remaining ingredients together, season, and pour over the celeriac.

Cover with foil and bake for 40 minutes, then remove the foil, compress the celeriac a little, and cook for a further 20–30 minutes until the cream is thick, the celeriac tender and the surface golden.

Serves 4

---

700 g/1 lb 9 oz celeriac (1 average-
   sized root)
sea salt and freshly ground black pepper
225 ml/8 fl oz double cream
50 ml/2 fl oz white wine
$\frac{1}{3}$ teaspoon mild curry spice

Red Pepper and Celeriac Charlotte

This is the apple type of charlotte: top and bottom lined with slices of bread dabbed with melted butter that crisp up beautifully in the process of baking, while inside are roasted peppers, a purée of celeriac and a layer of Fontina cheese. This is fairly rich and substantial, so serve it as a main course with a salad before or after.

Preheat the oven to 200°C fan oven/220°C or 425°F electric oven/ Gas 7. Remove the cores and seeds from the peppers and cut into wide strips. Place in a roasting dish, scatter over the garlic, season generously, pour over the oil and roast for 30–40 minutes until beginning to caramelize at the edges.

While the peppers are cooking, prepare the celeriac purée. Bring a large pan of water to the boil and acidulate it with the lemon juice. Slice the skin from the celeriac roots and cut them into pieces. Boil for 15 minutes until tender, then drain and purée in a food processor with the crème fraîche, and season with nutmeg, salt, pepper and lemon juice.

Select a baking dish approximately 30.5 × 23 cm/12 × 9 inches, and 5 cm/2 inches deep. Using a pastry brush, dab the bread generously on one side with the butter. Cover the base of the dish with slices so that there is a small overlap, and paint the topsides with butter. Lay the peppers over the base, then the Fontina, and spread the celeriac purée on top. Lay another layer of overlapping slices of bread on the surface, again painting with butter on both sides.

Bake for 20 minutes in the preheated oven, then reduce the heat to 170°C fan oven/180°C or 350°F electric oven/Gas 4 and bake for a further 20 minutes until the surface is lightly golden and crisp. Serve straight away.

Photograph between pages 56 and 57.

Serves 4–6

approx. ¾ large loaf of thinly sliced white bread, crusts removed
175–300 g/6–10½ oz unsalted butter, melted
225 g/8 oz Fontina cheese, sliced

Peppers
700 g/1 lb 9 oz red peppers (approx. 5)
2 garlic cloves, peeled and finely chopped
sea salt and freshly ground black pepper
2 tablespoons extra virgin olive oil

Celeriac purée
juice of ½ lemon
1.35 kg/3 lb celeriac (2 average-sized roots)
150 ml/5 fl oz crème fraîche
freshly grated nutmeg
sea salt and freshly ground black pepper
lemon juice for seasoning

Spiced Celeriac Mash

➤ Bring a large pan of salted water to the boil and acidulate it with half the lemon juice. Peel the celeriac and potatoes and cut into pieces. Boil for 15–17 minutes until tender, drain and press through a sieve or a mouli-légumes.

While the vegetables are cooking, chop the garlic and crush to a paste with a sprinkling of salt, using the flat edge of a knife. Heat 4 tablespoons of the olive oil in a small saucepan and cook the garlic, cumin and cayenne momentarily until nicely aromatic – the garlic must not colour. Immediately stir this into the vegetable purée, adjust the salt, season with pepper, and add some of the remaining lemon juice to taste.

Rewarm the purée before serving it. Coarsely crush the coriander seeds in a pestle and mortar. Heat the remaining olive oil in a small saucepan, cook the seeds for a minute or two until they begin to colour, then spoon over the warm mash.

Serves 4

juice of 1 lemon
900 g/2 lb celeriac
900 g/2 lb maincrop potatoes
3 garlic cloves, peeled
sea salt
5 tablespoons extra virgin olive oil
¾ teaspoon ground cumin
pinch of cayenne
freshly ground black pepper
1 level teaspoon coriander seeds

Other Ideas

➤ Serve a beetroot purée and a celeriac purée together on a plate as a starter, with croûtons and a sprinkling of parsley: once each vegetable is cooked, purée them separately with crème fraîche, butter and seasoning, and a squeeze of lemon juice.

➤ Make a cream of celeriac soup by sweating carrots, leeks, a little turnip and celeriac in butter then cooking with vegetable stock. Purée, add plenty of cream, and serve it with croûtons spread with Stilton flashed under the grill.

➤ Serve a mound of celeriac mash with pan-fried mushrooms and their juices spooned over, and a sprinkling of parsley. Ideally use shiitake or wild mushrooms.

➤ Roast celeriac, carrots, parsnips, red peppers, aubergines and whole heads of garlic together as a selection of vegetables.

➤ Arrange a selection of hors d'oeuvres consisting of radishes, olives or caper berries, potato salad, quail's eggs, rémoulade and mushrooms à la grècque.

See also:

Roasted Root Vegetables with Rocket Pesto (page 130)

Chicory

Of the many different chicories, the ones we are all familiar with are the 'Witloof' chicons, or Belgian chicory, those tightly closed buds, blanched to the palest of greens. Forcing 'Witloof' chicons in the dark renders tender heads that are an enticing blend of bitter and sweet. I once ate a salad at the Criterion brasserie in Piccadilly, under the auspices of Marco Pierre White, that consisted of a plateful of separated chicory leaves with a walnut dressing and creamy chunks of blue cheese; it was a beautifully stark rendition.

Radicchio, on the other hand (or radiochi as my corner shop puts it), I have almost given up on in salads; one too many super-acerbic heads has put me off. At most I like just a few leaves in a mixture. It is capable of extraordinary bitterness, which is unpredictable, and it was when a large plate of chargrilled radicchio with shavings of Parmesan hit the bin that I was finally convinced to stick to braising it.

When used in a risotto, braised or slowly wilted, radicchio changes character completely, becoming slippery and luscious, while the bitterness is subdued and very appealing. The downside is that the rich vermilion which attracted you in the first place turns to a muddy red. But this is a small price to pay for a vegetable that salutes the bitterness of other ingredients such as olives, Vacherin, Seville orange juice and more curiously beer, as you will see below.

'Witloof' chicons cook up beautifully too. Slice them finely and sweat them in butter, add a dash of white wine and cook to reduce it. Then cover with double cream, season, and cook over a low heat until you are left with a thick, creamy purée, a fraction of the original volume, that is utterly delectable. You can use this purée to fill a hollowed-out squash before baking it, or be very unseasonal and fill a cooked globe artichoke heart and top with a poached egg or sautéed mushrooms. I have also used it as the base for eggs mollet, and underneath grilled fillets of sole and seared scallops. Alternatively, stir some grainy mustard into it to serve with guinea fowl or chicken, and some leeks.

This purée makes good use of the larger heads: chicons come in many varying sizes. And you will require small heads should you want to encase them in a thin blanket of air-dried ham before baking them with a béchamel sauce. But you can always cut down large heads by removing the outer leaves and keeping these for some other use.

The Northern Italians take their chicory very seriously indeed. According to Anna del Conte, in *The Classic Food of Northern Italy*, they have three favourite varieties: 'Treviso', 'Verona' and 'Castelfranco'. I remember 'Red Treviso' as being an integral part of Trento market – that and the long trestle tables piled with different varieties of wild mushroom. 'Red Treviso' is long and spindly, and it does occasionally present itself in better greengrocers here. It is in fact a pink version of 'Witloof', and not overly bitter. Wilted and then braised with pulses, it forms, I believe, its most successful marriage: the dry, sweet and mealy beans with faintly bitter, silky leaves.

It was Sally Clarke, owner of the

Californian-inspired restaurant Clarke's in Kensington, who alerted me to the notion of wilting chicory and endive some years back – this makes especially good use of any outer leaves and you can use curly endive, broad-leaved escarole, Belgian chicory or 'Red Treviso'. Wilt them in a frying pan with butter or olive oil, some garlic and seasoning, and serve as an accompanying vegetable.

The bitterness of these winter leaves, incidentally, is supposed to be addictive, or at least acquired as a taste. And I can remember when I didn't like olives.

Selection

For Belgian chicory, look for heads that are pale green and tightly closed – if they have begun to open at the top then they are past their best. Store them in a paper bag in the bottom of the fridge.

Preparation

When preparing chicory it rapidly discolours, so cut and cook it as quickly as possible. A squeeze of lemon juice when you are cooking it will preserve its colour.

Braised Radicchio and Chickpeas

This would be good eaten with a youngish goat's cheese and some crusty bread. Were you to turn a blind eye and open a tin of chickpeas it qualifies as fast – but there is a difference in quality.

Place the soaked chickpeas in a large saucepan with plenty of water, bring to the boil and simmer until tender for about 1¼ hours. Leave to cool in the water, then drain.

Trim the radicchio, removing any damaged outer leaves, and cut into segments about 1 cm/½ inch wide. Heat the olive oil in a large saucepan and sweat the radicchio until it turns a dull red and begins to colour. Add the chilli, garlic, orange zest, bay leaf, chickpeas, wine and tomatoes, bring to a simmer, cover and cook over a low heat for 15 minutes – stir half-way through, mashing the tomatoes down. The chickpeas and radicchio should be sitting in a small amount of well-flavoured liquor. Discard the orange zest, bay leaf and garlic and cool for about 10 minutes.

Season, stir in the orange and lemon juice, and add the olives. Serve warm or at room temperature, with the olive oil poured over and a scattering of parsley.

Serves 4

175 g/6 oz chickpeas, soaked overnight
    in 4 times their volume of water
2 heads radicchio
3 tablespoons extra virgin olive oil
½ teaspoon finely chopped red chilli
3 garlic cloves, peeled
5 cm/2 inch strip of orange zest
1 bay leaf
150 ml/5 fl oz white wine
200 g/7 oz tomatoes, skinned and
    chopped
sea salt and freshly ground black pepper

To serve
1 tablespoon orange juice
1 tablespoon lemon juice or Seville
    orange juice
70 g/2½ oz black olives, pitted and
    halved
6 tablespoons extra virgin olive oil
coarsely chopped flat-leaved parsley

Radicchio-filled Pancakes with a White Beer Sauce

The icing on the cake would be a few drops of black or white truffle oil added at the table. Use an unassertive beer such as the excellent Hoegaarden, which is mild enough to appeal to non-beer-drinkers like myself.

In a bowl whisk together all the ingredients for the pancakes except for the melted butter: leave to stand for 30 minutes, then add this too.

While the batter is resting make the sauce: melt the butter in a medium-sized heavy-bottomed saucepan, add the flour and cook for 1–2 minutes. Combine the cream, milk, stock and wine and gradually whisk into the roux. Return to the heat and cook, stirring, until it thickens. Cover and simmer over a low heat for 30 minutes. Season and add the beer.

The quickest way to cook the pancakes is to use 2 frying pans. You may need to grease the pans initially with vegetable oil, but thereafter the butter in the batter should be sufficient. Cook them over a medium heat, ladling the batter into each frying pan so the base is lightly coated. The pancakes should be 18–20.5 cm/7–8 inches in diameter; after a minute or two, when the top is completely dry, turn them over and cook the other side. Stack on a plate.

Remove the outer leaves from the radicchio, halve, cut out tough stalks and slice thinly. Melt the butter in a frying pan and sweat the radicchio until it has turned dull in colour and is limp.

Preheat the oven to 190°C fan oven/200°C or 400°F electric oven/ Gas 6. Roll up the pancakes with some of the radicchio and cheese in each one and lay them side by side in a gratin or shallow baking dish. Pour over the sauce and bake for 20–30 minutes, until the sauce has turned golden in patches.

Serves 4 (12 pancakes)

Pancakes
175 g/6 oz plain flour
pinch each of sea salt and sugar
300 ml/½ pint milk
150 ml/5 fl oz water
2 medium eggs, plus 2 egg yolks
40 g/1½ oz melted butter

Sauce
25 g/1 oz unsalted butter
20 g/¾ oz plain flour
150 ml/5 fl oz double cream
150 ml/5 fl oz milk
200 ml/7 fl oz vegetable stock
100 ml/3½ fl oz white wine
sea salt and freshly ground black pepper
50 ml/2 fl oz white beer

Filling
2 heads radicchio
25 g/1 oz unsalted butter
175 g/6 oz Vacherin, or very ripe Brie
   (weight excluding rind)

Gratin of Chicory and Haricot Beans with Bay

The first time I made this I was spoilt with fresh haricot or 'coco' beans in the Camargue. These have a smoothness that you rarely find in dried beans, and delicate skins, but in this country I'm afraid we have to make do with dried ones. Pulses and chicory are extremely good together, whether as here, or in a salad.

Place the soaked beans in a medium-sized saucepan and cover with water by 5 cm/2 inches. Bring to the boil and cook for 2 minutes, drain, cover with cold water again, bring back to the boil and simmer until tender (1–1½ hours). If necessary top up with boiling water. Place the pan under the cold tap and run water into it until the beans are cool, then drain them and place in a gratin dish (or other shallow ovenproof dish).

Trim the base of the chicory, halve the heads and slice lengthwise into strips. Heat the butter in a frying pan and sweat the chicory until it turns translucent and begins to colour, seasoning it. Mix it in with the haricots. Peel and deseed the tomato and cut it into strips.

Preheat the oven to 200°C fan oven/220°C or 425°F electric oven/Gas 7. Place the crème fraîche, vegetable stock, tomato, garlic, bay leaf and seasoning in a small saucepan and bring to the boil. Pour this over the haricots and chicory and bake for 25–30 minutes until lightly coloured on the surface.

Serves 4

140 g/5 oz dried haricot beans, soaked overnight
3 chicory heads
20 g/³⁄₄ oz unsalted butter
sea salt and freshly ground black pepper
1 × 175 g/6 oz tomato
200 ml/7 fl oz crème fraîche
50 ml/2 fl oz vegetable stock
1 garlic clove, peeled and finely chopped
1 bay leaf, torn into 3 pieces

Chicory and Avocado Caesar Salad

I have mixed feelings about playing around with a salad as perfect as a Caesar, but chicory, like cos lettuce, is an ideal blend of crisp stalk and leaf, and avocado makes a voluptuous partner. You could add another darker salad leaf as well to give it a bit of colour. The Parmesan should be finely grated as opposed to powdered.

First prepare the dressing: bring a small pan of water to the boil, cook the eggs for 1 minute, remove and cool them under cold running water then shell them into a liquidizer, scooping out the cooked white that lines the inside of the shell. Add the remaining ingredients for the dressing and whizz to a pale and creamy emulsion.

Cut the bread into 1 cm/½ inch cubes. Heat enough olive oil in a frying pan to shallow-fry the bread, add the cubes and cook, tossing constantly, until they are golden and crisp. Remove and cool on absorbent paper.

To serve the salad, slice the bottoms off the chicory heads, remove any damaged outer leaves and separate the remainder. Arrange these on a large serving plate. Halve the avocados and extract the stones, incise the skin into quarters and peel it off, then slice the halves into thin strips. Mix these in with the chicory.

Pour over the dressing and lightly mix in the Parmesan. Scatter the croûtons over and serve straight away.

Photograph opposite page 57.

Serves 4

Dressing
2 medium eggs
½ garlic clove, peeled and chopped
2 tablespoons lemon juice
2 teaspoons Worcestershire sauce
150 ml/5 fl oz extra virgin olive oil
sea salt and freshly ground black pepper

Salad
2 large slices of white bread, 1 cm/
 ½ inch thick
olive oil for frying
450 g/1 lb small 'Witloof' chicons (Belgian
 endive)
3 avocados
60 g/2 oz freshly grated Parmesan

Other Ideas

➤ On account of its sweetness, a balsamic vinaigrette is perfect for a chicory and bean salad.

➤ Include just a few strips of radicchio in a green salad, a couple of sweet lettuces, and some spicy leaves such as rocket or watercress – this will give a good balance.

➤ Belgian chicory heads can be opened up and stuffed, then tied to secure them, and braised.

➤ Wilt chicory in olive oil with a little garlic, then add a dash of cream, a few drops of brandy, and stir in some cubes of blue cheese so they just begin to melt as it is served – delicious with thin, crispy toast.

➤ Halve chicory heads and sauté in butter, then arrange them in a gratin dish, pour over double cream with a touch of white wine, and bake in the oven until the surface is golden.

See also:

Gratin of Cauliflower with Crème Fraîche, Capers and Lemon (page 54)

Chillies

Not so long ago it seemed as though a chilli invasion was imminent. Picking up from Santa Fe and the American line in south-western cooking, we were to have pale yellow 'chawas', chocolate-coloured 'chili pasillas', smoky 'poblanos' and dimpled orange 'manzanas'. I, for one, am breathing a sigh of relief that it hasn't really happened. Chillies are a fascinating group, but en masse the quest for fire smacked of fad.

There are so many chillies and derivative products, it is far better to whittle the business down to a skeletal basis, mastering the art of using just one or two types rather than trying to get to grips with using a different chilli for every recipe you cook. And believe me there is one. There are hundreds of varieties, with differing characteristics. For the cook, the two essentials of fresh chillies are heat and flavour. Heat is the most widely documented of the two facets, scientifically quoted in Scoville units.

Scoville units are named after one Wilbur Scoville, and I am convinced he would have hung out with the likes of Ernest Hemingway in Havana in the dying days of the Batista regime, indulging in ritual feasts of prawns thrown live on to the grill, macerated shell-on, the debris indelicately spat around the bar floor. The Scoville unit has machismo. By definition it is the dilution required to reach the threshold of taste. In lay terms the infamous habanero or Scotch bonnet has 100,000–300,000 Scoville units, while that sweet, friendly pussycat the red bell pepper has none at all.

Capsaicin, an oily substance, is present in the seeds and membranes of the chilli family. And as anyone who has ever ignored the golden rule to wear rubber gloves when chopping chillies knows, once burnt, twice shy. Some chillies are now marked with their heat scale, not in Scoville units, but as 'mild', 'hot' and 'very hot'. Which is sensible labelling. I steer clear of the searingly hot habaneros in favour of the milder jalapeños, whose heat is easier to control.

More than providing a real kick in a dish, just $\frac{1}{2}$ or 1 level teaspoon of minced chilli will give it a beautiful rounded piquancy that you cannot get from pepper. Increasingly I opt for a little chilli over pepper, not just in Eastern dishes, but in Mediterranean olive oil-based recipes too.

Used whole in stews, braises and casseroles is where flavour comes into play. It is essential that the chillies are in no way damaged, otherwise the heat from the seeds and membranes will leak out. The idea is to extract their fragrance, which is subtle but quite defined, and you discard the chilli once it is cooked. Mexicans would steep a whole bunch of them in the stew. That's knowhow.

Likewise, when I am roasting vegetables, I have got into the habit of tucking not only a few garlic cloves in here and there, but a couple of whole chillies as well, which will perfume the roasting juices, especially when slow-roasting tomatoes.

When it comes to by-products, I reckon that Tabasco and cayenne pepper cover me for most eventualities. Cayenne pepper or any other ground chilli powder should be fresh – this is a spice, and as such it deteriorates. They provide heat rather than flavour, but there are times where only cayenne pepper will do. I used to find it confusing that as well as Tabasco there is an enormous range of hot pepper sauces, the avenging liquors: kick ass, red devil, mother of all sauces, etc., and frankly they all do the same thing.

A precautionary tale

My experience of chilli burn as an unsuspecting novice was of sitting in a bath in excruciating pain after I had liberally smeared eyes, neck and face with invisible traces of chilli oil while preparing them. Even for a half teaspoonful of finely chopped chilli I now wear rubber gloves.

For small amounts of raw chilli do not worry about removing the skin – it is only in large quantities that it becomes evident. If you are roasting them, as with peppers the skin should slip off with ease.

Aubergine Yam Tart

This is a light tart: a base of crisp filo pastry layers with grilled aubergine slices dressed with a tart hot and sour Thai dressing known as 'Yam'.

Slice the aubergines lengthwise 0.75 cm/⅓ inch thick. Heat a griddle (or you could use a dry cast-iron frying pan), paint one side of the slices with olive oil and grill lightly until beginning to colour, but do not cook thoroughly. Paint the topside of the slices with oil, season, turn and grill likewise. Repeat with the remaining slices and reserve.

Preheat the oven to 190°C fan oven/200°C or 400°F electric oven/ Gas 6. Layer the filo sheets on a baking tray, painting each one generously with the melted butter. Lay the aubergine slices in rows on top of the filo pastry so that the slices overlap lengthwise. Cook for 20–25 minutes, until the filo pastry is golden and crisp and the aubergine nicely roasted. Remove and cool to room temperature.

While the tart is cooking make the dressing: cook the shallot, chilli and garlic in a dry frying pan until limp and beginning to colour. Finely chop and blend with the soy sauce, water, lemon juice and sugar. Spoon the dressing over the tart immediately before serving, and scatter over the sesame seeds.

Photograph opposite page 80.

Serves 4

2 medium aubergines (approx. 600 g/
   1 lb 4 oz)
extra virgin olive oil
sea salt and freshly ground black pepper
8 sheets of ready-made filo pastry
   23 × 30.5 cm/9 × 12 inches
80 g/3 oz unsalted butter, melted
3 shallots, peeled and chopped
1 heaped teaspoon medium hot chopped
   red chilli
2 garlic cloves, peeled and chopped
1 tablespoon light soy sauce
1 tablespoon water
2 tablespoons lemon juice
1 teaspoon sugar
1 level tablespoon sesame seeds,
   toasted in a dry frying pan

Potatoes with Onion in Olive Oil

This is a spicy medley of potatoes and onions. You could serve it with a meaty fish like tuna or swordfish, with grilled chicken, or as it is.

Bring a large pan of salted water to the boil. Slice the potatoes about 0.25 cm/⅛ inch thick and rinse in a sink of cold water to remove the starch. Cook the potatoes when the sauce is nearly ready: boil them for 2½ minutes, drain, then arrange the slices on 4 large plates and season with salt and pepper.

Heat the olive oil in a medium-sized saucepan and cook the onions for 6–8 minutes over a moderate heat until soft and beginning to caramelize at the edges, adding the garlic and chilli half-way through, and the parsley a minute before the end. Add the vinegar and cook this off. Spoon over the potatoes and serve immediately.

Serves 4

700 g/1 lb 9 oz new potatoes
sea salt and freshly ground black pepper
8 tablespoons extra virgin olive oil
2 red onions, peeled, halved and sliced
2 garlic cloves, peeled and finely chopped
1 heaped teaspoon medium hot red chilli, finely chopped
4 tablespoons small parsley sprigs
2 tablespoons red wine vinegar

Spaghetti with Red Pepper Pesto

This is a lovely fragrant pesto made with roasted peppers and chilli, which can be eaten in plentiful amounts.

Make the pesto first. Preheat the oven to 200°C fan oven/220°C or 425°F electric oven/Gas 7 and roast the peppers and the chilli for 20 minutes. Place one plastic carrier bag inside another, place the roasted peppers and chilli inside, secure the opening and leave them to cool. Slip the skins off the peppers and remove the seeds, washing as necessary under a cold tap. Skin the chilli, and reserve ½ teaspoon of the flesh.

Place the garlic cloves, basil and nuts in the bowl of a food processor and reduce to a coarse paste. Add the oil, the skinned peppers, chilli and seasoning, and process to a smooth pesto.

To serve, bring a large pan of salted water to the boil and cook the spaghetti, leaving it firm to the bite. Drain and toss it with a little olive oil, the pesto and seasoning. Mound into bowls and serve with Parmesan if wished.

Photograph between pages 80 and 81.

Serves 4

450 g/1 lb spaghetti
dash of extra virgin olive oil
sea salt and freshly ground black pepper

Pesto
3 red peppers
1 red chilli
2 garlic cloves, peeled
25 g/1 oz basil leaves
70 g/2½ oz roasted hazelnuts
2 tablespoons extra virgin olive oil
sea salt and freshly ground black pepper

To serve
freshly grated Parmesan (optional)

Other Ideas

➤ When making dhal I usually add a couple of whole red chillies for flavour, extracting them at the end.

➤ When making a rouille for serving with fish soup, roast a red chilli along with the red peppers and include a little of the roasted flesh in the sauce.

➤ When poaching pears I include a whole chilli in the spiced syrup, along with a cinnamon stick, green cardamom pods, a bay leaf, a strip of lemon zest and coriander seeds.

➤ 'Fire and ice' is a Californian creation of chilled melon in a syrup marinated with chopped chilli, then strained: the effect is exactly as its name suggests. Make a basic syrup by heating together water, sugar and a little chopped chilli, and cooling it. Add some lemon juice to taste, combine with the melon and chill it for about 12 hours.

➤ No salsa would be complete without its fair share of chilli, and of chopped raw onion and lime juice.

➤ Make a spicy mashed potato by cooking a chopped onion in vegetable oil until it is golden and adding ¾ teaspoon of chopped green chilli and ½ teaspoon each of cumin, mustard seeds and turmeric. Then add 1.2 kg/2 lb 12 oz of cooked mashed potato and fry for about 5 minutes.

See also:

Warm Salad of Roasted Aubergine, Tomatoes and Cannellini Beans (page 15)
Oriental Stir-fried Broccoli and Cauliflower (page 37)
Escabeche with Thyme Toast (page 38)
Oriental Late Summer Salad (page 51)
Braised Radicchio and Chickpeas (page 65)
Fennel à la Grècque (page 78)

Fennel

I once went foraging in the countryside just north of London with Gennaro Contaldo, Antonio Carluccio's procurer of all things wild for the Neal Street Restaurant. Just as a shopper knows exactly where to buy each ingredient, Gennaro had it all mapped out. At one point we came to a grinding halt on the driveway approach to a modern school, and there were several wild fennel plants, about 3 feet in height. Gennaro whipped out his knife and lopped off a tall branch, then peeled it. This was to be cooked like asparagus for serving with fish back at the restaurant.

The green foliage and thin green stalks are the other prized parts of the plant, and transport me immediately to Provence: red mullet grilled over sprigs of fennel. The feathery fronds can be chopped and used like dill – it is not dissimilar, coming from the same family. The tiny yellow flowers too can be used.

Wild fennel is tenacious and can become a pest in gardens, so I will not advise you to plant any. But it is easily recognizable in the wild, so try to locate a bush if you are interested in cooking with it. And don't tell anyone where it is.

It is Florence fennel, the cultivated bulb, that is the main concern here. This consists of leaf bases, and is made up of a series of sheaths. Perhaps it is because fennel marries so well with fish that I tend to think in terms of similar flavour combinations. It is a rule of thumb that seems to work.

Fennel can be eaten raw or cooked. At its simplest I have been served raw fennel at the end of dinner in Italy, but I prefer it at the beginning of a meal, sliced finely for dipping into tapenade or a goat's cheese dip. Or made into a little salad dressed with olive oil, lemon juice and seasoning, perhaps with a few orange segments added.

The outer layers tend to be tough, but these can be turned into soups and purées. A favourite soup is fennel and almond, thickened with ground almonds. Fennel brandade too: a warm, creamy purée of fennel and potato, with olive oil, cream, lemon juice and garlic (see page 158). You can eat this either with samphire strewn over the top, or with triangular croûtons. It makes a perfect bed for a roasted slab of white fish such as cod or halibut.

It has become popular to grill fennel on a ridged griddle or a barbecue – it can then be eaten with thin shavings of Parmesan, or mixed in with other roasted vegetables like aubergine, courgettes and peppers. Or it can be marinated with olive oil, lemon juice and a little lemon zest, some chilli and chopped fennel fronds or dill, and eaten with olives, sun-dried tomatoes, slices of Pecorino, radishes, quail's eggs, caper berries and so forth.

When fennel is braised it cooks to a deliciously succulent, silky consistency. The bulbs are best when they are a middling size, though this said, the small, flat bulbs can be eaten whole, and they will be deliciously tender and fragrant, braised with a little stock, some butter or olive oil and herbs like thyme, sage and oregano, and some garlic.

Preparation

I remember being confounded by the first specimens of fennel I had to chop. First they need trimming: take a thin slice off the base and cut off the shoots so they are level with the top of the bulb. If the bulbs are of a fair size, remove the outer sheaths, one or two depending on the size of the bulb. Reserve all these trimmings for soups and purées.

The bulbs can then either be quartered and cored, or halved, cored and thinly sliced. For diced fennel, halve the bulbs lengthwise, make a number of cuts from the top to just above the base, then do this at a right angle, then cut the fennel into dice. If not using the fennel straight away, reserve it in water that has been acidulated with lemon juice or vinegar.

Haricot Bean and Fennel Stew

This makes the perfect base for monkfish or some other white fish: add this to the casserole 10-15 minutes before it comes out of the oven. The vegetarian version is just grown-up baked beans and met with the approval of my six-year-old – one who knows.

Drain and rinse the beans, place in a saucepan and cover with cold water by 5 cm/2 inches. Bring to the boil, cook for 2 minutes and drain them, then cover with cold water again, bring back to the boil and simmer until tender, but do not boil vigorously. If necessary top up with boiling water during cooking. The cooking time will depend on the type of bean and how fresh they are – supermarket beans take about 1–1½ hours. Do not salt the beans until the end of cooking, otherwise the skins will toughen. To avoid the skins cracking once they are cooked, place the pan under the cold tap and run water into it until the beans are cool, then drain them.

Preheat the oven to 160°C fan oven/170°C or 325°F electric oven/ Gas 3. Cut off the fennel shoots, trim the base and cut the bulb into segments. Arrange the beans in a casserole with the fennel and the remaining ingredients, except the seasoning, crème fraîche and parsley. Cover and cook in the oven for 2 hours, checking towards the end to make sure they have not dried out – if necessary add more liquid.

Season the stew, then remove the beans and vegetables to a warm serving bowl, discarding the herbs. Stir the crème fraîche into the juices and reduce on the stove top until slightly thickened: pour the sauce over the beans and check the seasoning. Serve in bowls, with parsley scattered over.

Serves 3–4

---

250 g/9 oz haricot beans, soaked overnight
1 large fennel bulb
450 g/1 lb tomatoes, peeled, seeded and diced
2 bay leaves
2 sprigs of rosemary
4 garlic cloves, peeled
a large pinch of saffron filaments (approx. 25)
150 ml/5 fl oz white wine or vermouth
600 ml/1 pint vegetable stock, or bean cooking water
3 tablespoons extra virgin olive oil
sea salt and freshly ground black pepper
3 heaped tablespoons crème fraîche

To serve
chopped flat-leaved parsley

Fennel à la Grècque

Trim the fennel bulbs of their shoots and outer sheaths, and either quarter or cut into six so each segment remains attached by the root. Make an aromatic broth by combining all the remaining ingredients (except those to serve) in a pan; contain the seeds in a small square of muslin. Bring the broth to the boil and simmer, covered, for 10 minutes.

Add the fennel, bring back to the boil, cover the pan, turn the heat down low and simmer for 45 minutes, stirring occasionally, until the fennel is very tender and a knife can be inserted easily. Remove the fennel to a bowl and reduce the remaining liquor to several tablespoons. Strain the reduced liquor over the fennel. Allow to cool. Add the remaining olive oil, sharpen with lemon juice, adjust the seasoning and add the olives and tomato.

Serves 4

4 fennel bulbs
300 ml/½ pint water
5 tablespoons extra virgin olive oil
juice of ½ lemon
½ teaspoon sea salt
1 pinch of saffron filaments (about 20)
1 shallot, peeled and finely chopped
6 parsley stalks
5 sprigs of thyme
1 whole medium hot red chilli
12 black peppercorns
¼ teaspoon fennel seeds
6 coriander seeds

To serve
3 tablespoons extra virgin olive oil
lemon juice
sea salt and freshly ground black pepper
70 g/2½ oz black olives, pitted
1 beefsteak tomato, skinned, seeded
  and diced

Fennel Soup with Ditalini

This is a thick, creamy soup with a very delicate flavour, served with a garnish of olive oil and snipped chives. Ditalini are small tubular pasta used for soups. I buy one made by Barilla called 'ditalini rigati', which are ridged, but there are any number of tiny pastas that could double up.

Heat the butter and oil in a large saucepan and sweat the vegetables over a medium heat until soft and translucent: you will need to do this in 2 batches. Return all the vegetables to the pan. Add the wine and reduce to a syrup. Add the vegetable stock, star anise, lemon zest and seasoning and simmer covered for 20 minutes. Remove the star anise (it may have broken up so search thoroughly for stray bits). Now liquidize the soup, pass through a sieve and liquidize again: return to a clean saucepan. You can prepare the soup to this point in advance, but if you reheat it you may need to add a little more vegetable stock to thin it to the right consistency.

Bring a pan of salted water to the boil, cook the pasta according to the packet instructions leaving it firm to the bite, then drain. While the pasta is cooking, reheat the soup, stir in the Pernod and lemon juice and adjust the seasoning. Add the pasta to the soup and serve in bowls with a drizzle of oil and plenty of snipped chives.

Photograph opposite page 81.

Serves 4

25 g/1 oz unsalted butter
2 tablespoons extra virgin olive oil
900 g/2 lb fennel, trimmed and chopped
2 sticks celery, sliced
175 g/6 oz carrot, peeled and sliced
150 ml/5 fl oz white wine
750 ml/1½ pints vegetable stock
2 star anise
zest of I lemon
sea salt and freshly ground black pepper
70 g/2½ oz ditalini or other small pasta
2 tablespoons Pernod or other pastis
a few drops of lemon juice

To serve
extra virgin olive oil
snipped chives

Other Ideas

➤ Accentuate any fennel preparation with fennel seeds, chopped fennel fronds or flowers, a pastis liqueur such as Ricard or Pernod, and chopped dill and dill seeds.

➤ Braise whole young fennel bulbs, or quarters of larger ones, with olive oil, a little white wine and water or vegetable stock, and garlic – by the end of cooking the liquor should have amalgamated into a thickened sauce. Stir in diced tomato and a squeeze of lemon juice.

➤ Creamed fennel will serve as a filling for all manner of things, from cooked artichoke hearts to baked potatoes. Sweat diced fennel in butter until it is nice and soft, add a slug of white wine and cook to reduce this, then cover with double cream and cook slowly until it coats the fennel in a thick cream sauce.

➤ Make a salad of fine shavings of fennel and red pepper, fine slivers of black olive, and dress with a balsamic vinaigrette.

➤ Make an oriental-style braised fennel with aromatics such as lemon grass, fresh ginger, garlic and chilli. Add some chopped coriander before serving.

➤ Cook some macaroni, then brown slivers of fennel in olive oil, add some toasted pine-nuts and flaked almonds, some currants soaked in boiling water for 10 minutes, and a little saffron ground and blended with a dessertspoon of boiling water. Toss the macaroni into the frying pan and at the end add lots of crisp, fried breadcrumbs. You could also add chopped wild fennel.

See also:

Cream of Mushroom Soup (page 121)
Fennel Brandade with Samphire (page 158)
Tomatoes Flambéed in Pastis, with Fennel and Feta (page 191)

Aubergine Yam Tart (page 71)

Spaghetti with Red Pepper Pesto (page 73)

Polenta with Stilton and French Beans (page 94)

Garlic

There are numerous varieties of garlic, ranging from the size of a plum to the size of your fist, from parchment white to shades of pink. But for many cooks it is the purple-skinned types typical of Provence that are considered to be the finest.

We are so used to having garlic to hand all year round that it is easy to lose sight of it as a seasonal crop, but spring in the Mediterranean is greeted with fresh green 'new season' garlic. Basically all garlic is green immediately prior to harvesting, at which point it hasn't developed its full strength of flavour. Unlike ordinary garlic, with its papery husks, fresh garlic has not been dried out, so the stem is succulent and the outer skin fleshy. When you break into a head of fresh garlic it seems to be an endless succession of skins which cook up much like a shallot, so one does not have to worry too much about removing them all. While the flavour is milder than that of the ordinary garlic, it is superbly clean and sharp. There is a distinctly musty savour about the ordinary that is not present in the fresh.

There are certain dishes where only the ordinary, dried-out garlic will do: an aïoli, for example, where the whole point is to succumb to its uncooked, iron grip and sense that bite in the back of your throat. Likewise, all those garlic-heavy soups where the cloves change perfume altogether as they simmer to a silky soft button; here again you require that depth.

Fresh garlic is wonderfully perky, particularly good in gazpacho, and in a garlicky vinaigrette to dress a nice butch lettuce, such as cos, with some croûtons and Parmesan. Also in that zesty all-rounder gremolata, a blend of freshly chopped parsley, lemon zest and garlic. This is sometimes sprinkled over osso buco, which is not to my personal taste, but its use goes further for enlivening cooked fish and warm pulses dressed with olive oil.

The important thing when cooking with garlic is not to burn it, otherwise it becomes bitter. If frying, either add it to a pan along with other ingredients, or add it about 15 seconds before adding something else: it burns very quickly. It is worth remembering that when you want to dim the sensation of garlic, it can be blanched in boiling water. Also the greater the surface of garlic that is exposed the greater the pungency, which is one reason for crushing rather than chopping it. Preferable to the business of rubbing a bowl with a clove of garlic, which I find leaves a fairly imperceptible trace, is to crush a whole clove to a paste, smear this around the bowl or pan and then scrape it off; this gives a realistic suggestion.

If you have a problem with the notorious after-effect of smelling of garlic, then eating parsley, thyme, mint or basil will allegedly rid you of it. Not the easiest hypothesis to test. Consider instead its well-documented beneficial effects, the most notorious being the story of the 'vinegar of the four thieves': a herbal vinegar containing lots of garlic supposed to have protected four thieves from the plague in Marseilles in the 1720s as they robbed corpses.

I find all the dehydrated forms of garlic to be thoroughly offensive and the quickest way I can think of to ruin something. They are often used to spike shop-bought hummus and dips – something you realize too late, after eating them. The one exception to this is the seasoning for Louisiana blackened fish, a feisty blend of different powdered peppers, onion and garlic powder and dried herbs.

Puréeing garlic

Garlic's aroma comes from an oil released when a clove is cut, diallyl disulfide, which is why it is at its most pungent when it is crushed to a purée. Fresh garlic is juicy and does not purée as well as the ordinary, but do not let this put you off using it for a garlic butter. I am not a fan of garlic presses – the effort that goes into cleaning them effectively might as well be put into crushing the bulb with a knife. To do this, peel and coarsely chop the garlic, sprinkle it with salt and crush, using the flat edge of a knife. It should quickly liquefy to a pungent purée.

Fennel Soup with Ditalini (page 79)

Roasted Garlic

The wonderful combination of roasted garlic with goat's cheese is famously that of Alice Waters of Chez Panisse in California. You cannot better garlic heads roasted as below, then squeezed from their casing on to some rough-textured bread spread with a fresh goat's cheese blended with cream. But you can serve roasted garlic with any assortment of appetizers, with cured meats, cornichons and olives, or Middle Eastern vegetable and pulse purées.

You can also add a little roasted garlic purée to a mash of potato or pumpkin, or turn it into a creamy sauce for vegetables. When buying garlic it should be compact, and not sprouting. It is at its best at the beginning of the season. You can obtain special garlic pots with holes for ventilation, which also store it out of the light.

Preheat the oven to 140°C fan oven/150°C or 300°F electric oven/ Gas 2. Cut the top off each head of garlic to reveal the cloves and place in a shallow baking dish. Tuck the sprigs of thyme in here and there, season well, pour over the olive oil and dot with the butter. Cover with foil and cook for 1¼ hours, basting every so often. Serve warm, but not so it is too hot to handle.

Serves 4–6

6 heads of garlic
5 sprigs of thyme
sea salt and freshly ground black pepper
4 tablespoons extra virgin olive oil
25 g/1 oz unsalted butter

Forty Clove Soup with Thyme

A soup that shouts garlic – and it is the standard, strongly flavoured heads you require. As for the cook's lore about cooking a lot of garlic for a long time and it no longer tasting of garlic, it may change its perfume, but the end result still reeks, and you will find as I do that as this soup simmers away the kitchen becomes deliciously thick with it.

Place the herbs, garlic, lemon zest, wine and stock in a large saucepan. Bring to the boil and simmer uncovered for 30 minutes until it reduces by a quarter: skim as necessary. Remove and discard the herbs and zest, and purée the garlic cloves with a little of the soup in a liquidizer. Return the garlic mixture to the pan and season. Add the *beurre manié* and stir till melted, then simmer for a minute or two.

To serve, preheat the grill and reheat the soup. Arrange the goat's cheese slices on the toasted French bread and place under the grill until the cheese is turning golden. Pour the soup into 4 hot bowls, drizzle over the olive oil, and accompany with the goat's cheese toast.

Serves 4

6 branches of thyme (several twigs each branch)
1 bay leaf
40 garlic cloves, peeled
5 cm/2 inch strip of lemon zest
200 ml/7 fl oz white wine
1.65 litres/3 pints vegetable stock
sea salt and freshly ground black pepper
1 teaspoon *beurre manié* (equal quantities of plain flour and unsalted butter, blended together)
2 tablespoons extra virgin olive oil

To serve
8 × 1 cm/½ inch slices of French bread, lightly toasted and drizzled with extra virgin olive oil
150 g/5½ oz Crottin de Chavignol or similar goat's cheese, sliced

Tuscan Bread Salad

This salad is not of the chunky variety – everything is diced small. And the bread is crisp – I am not a fan of soggy lumps of it. You can add 175 g/6 oz of peeled prawns to this salad if you wish.

Heat the oven to 160°C fan oven/170°C or 325°F electric oven/Gas 3. Leave the crusts on the bread and cut into 0.5 cm/¼ inch dice. Lay these in a single layer on a baking sheet and cook in the oven until they dry out, without colouring, for about 7 minutes: leave to cool.

Peel, quarter and deseed the cucumber, and cut into 0.5 cm/¼ inch dice. Plunge the tomatoes into boiling water for 30 seconds, then into cold water. Slip off the skins, then quarter, deseed and dice them. Dice the onion. Place the diced vegetables, including the garlic, together in a bowl. Just before serving add the bread and basil to the salad, toss with the oil and lemon juice and season to taste.

Serves 4

---

100 g/3½ oz open-textured white bread, sliced 0.5 cm/¼ inch thick
¾ cucumber
700 g/1 lb 9 oz beefsteak tomatoes
25 g/1 oz red onion, peeled
1 garlic clove, peeled and finely chopped
1 heaped teaspoon shredded basil
5 tablespoons extra virgin olive oil
squeeze of lemon juice
sea salt and freshly ground black pepper

Other Ideas

➤ Dress spaghetti with extra virgin olive oil, chilli, garlic and parsley.

➤ Scatter a persillade of finely chopped garlic, parsley and lemon zest over warm chickpeas and diced celery dressed with olive oil and a squeeze of lemon juice.

➤ Squeeze out cloves of roasted garlic from their casing and stir them into scrambled eggs.

➤ Fill 'Little Gem' squashes with grated Gruyère, finely chopped garlic and cream and bake for 30 minutes in a hot oven.

➤ Bourride is one of the finest displays for garlic. As well as fish such as monkfish and sea bass, you can use a selection of vegetables – the real treat is the liquor, thickened with a garlic mayonnaise at the end.

➤ Bagna cauda is an almost instant fondue of garlic and anchovies with olive oil and butter for dipping raw vegetables. Melt 60 g/2 oz of unsalted butter over a very low heat, add 4 finely chopped garlic cloves, then 5 chopped anchovies and 175 ml/6 fl oz of olive oil, and cook until you have a smooth sauce. It is supposed to be kept warm over a spirit burner, but not having one shouldn't put you off.

See also:

Warm Salad of Roasted Aubergine, Tomatoes and Cannellini Beans (page 15)
Ten Minute Broad Bean Soup with Tapenade (page 33)
Oriental Stir-fried Broccoli and Cauliflower (page 37)
Escabeche with Thyme Toast (page 38)
Stuffed Cabbage with Porcini and Gruyère (page 42)
Provençal Hors d'Oeuvres (page 49)
Spiced Celeriac Mash (page 61)
Gratin of Chicory and Haricot Beans with Bay (page 67)

Aubergine Yam Tart (page 71)
Grilled Aubergine Slices in Ginger Marinade (page 89)
Lebanese Runner Beans (page 95)
Stoved Jerusalem Artichokes with Provençal Herbs (page 103)
Leek Dhal with Garlic Raita (page 113)
Potato and Emmental Gratin (page 148)
Swiss Chard and Sorrel Tart (page 184)

Ginger

Ginger I can vividly recall my first encounter with fresh ginger, on a visit to Thailand, where I had been on a week's trek in the Golden Triangle. (Perhaps I should mention that such activity is most out of character.) One afternoon as we stood at the base of some steep hills our guide looked upwards and pointed to a distant cave: our destination, to which we were cajoled, huffing and puffing. While recovering from this monumental climb our guide started scrambling around in the undergrowth, filling his pockets, with what I could not see.

Later that evening we stayed in a small village, where the guide prepared our dinner. The food I ate on this trek was the best Thai food I have ever eaten – all the cooking was performed with basic utensils over an open fire, in huts with mud floors. It was fresh ginger he had gathered at the cave, and with it he made the most wonderful spicy relish. Sadly I did not glean the recipe, but the flavour was not one that I have forgotten.

Ginger comes from a family that includes lesser and greater galangal and turmeric. The Asians use it fresh or pickled, and we extend this use to powdered and preserved. Fresh ginger is an extraordinary aromatic, clean, fresh and peppery. It suffers from the same curse as Jerusalem artichokes, that of having knobs which are all but impossible to peel, so choose nice plump roots. It is easy enough to recognize when ginger is past its best – it starts to shrivel. I would advise you to chuck it at that point. It also becomes fibrous as it ages.

I used to regard garlic as my failsafe flavouring, but these days I am lost without fresh ginger and chillies thrown in. And its

use extends beyond oriental cookery; it will fit neatly into all sorts of European dishes that don't usually include it.

Apart from when it is preserved in jars in syrup, I have never come across fresh ginger used as a vegetable, except for deep-fried strips, which are delicious. The two basic ways of using it are finely diced, or as a juice, which can be obtained from pressing the ginger in a garlic press.

Tomato, Watercress and Ginger Quiche

This is a shallow quiche-style tart — deliciously fragrant with thyme and ginger, and lightly set. Serve it with a salad. You can buy the pastry if you're short of time.

To make the pastry, place the flour, salt and butter in the bowl of a food processor and reduce to crumbs — you can also do this by hand. Bring the dough together with the egg, wrap it in clingfilm and rest in the fridge for 1 hour.

Preheat the oven to 180°C fan oven/190°C or 375°F electric oven/ Gas 5. On a lightly floured surface roll the pastry 0.25 cm/⅛ inch thick and line a shallow 23 cm/9 inch tart tin with a removable base allowing 0.5 cm/¼ inch for shrinkage — about a third of the pastry will be excess. Line with baking parchment and baking beans and bake the case for 15 minutes. Remove the paper and beans and return to the oven for 8 minutes until very lightly golden.

Skin the tomatoes by plunging them into boiling water for 30 seconds, then into cold water. Quarter and remove the seeds and slice the quarters into long strips. Heat the olive oil in a frying pan, add the garlic and ginger, and moments later add the thyme and watercress and cook until it wilts. Add the tomatoes, cook for a minute, then remove from the heat and season.

Whisk the egg yolks with the cream and seasoning and mix with the watercress and tomato mixture. Pour into the part-baked case and cook for 25 minutes. Serve at room temperature.

Serves 4 as a main course, 6 as a starter

Filling
450 g/1 lb tomatoes
2 tablespoons extra virgin olive oil
2 garlic cloves, peeled and finely
　chopped
2.5 cm/1 inch fresh ginger, peeled and
　finely chopped
1 heaped teaspoon thyme leaves
175 g/6 oz watercress, coarsely
　chopped
sea salt and freshly ground black pepper
3 medium egg yolks
150 ml/5 fl oz double cream

Pastry
225 g/8 oz plain flour
pinch of salt
125 g/4½ oz unsalted butter
1 medium egg

Grilled Aubergine Slices in Ginger Marinade

If you're in a hurry this can be eaten straight away, but it benefits from being left to steep for several hours at room temperature, by which time the aubergine literally melts as you eat it, impregnated with ginger, garlic and chilli.

I keep two types of griddle, a ridged and a flat one, and prefer to use the flat one for grilling aubergine, although a ridged one can be used. In their absence, use a cast-iron frying pan.

Heat a griddle and thinly slice the aubergines lengthwise, cutting at a slight angle. Brush one side of the slices with olive oil and grill until nicely mottled with brown. Brush the topside with oil, turn and cook on the other side. Reserve.

Combine all the ingredients for the marinade and layer with the aubergine slices in a shallow container. Cover and leave at room temperature until you are ready to eat. Serve with some of the marinade spooned over, and a spoon of tomato in the centre.

Serves 4 as a starter

2 aubergines
extra virgin olive oil for grilling

Marinade
8 tablespoons groundnut oil
3 tablespoons dark soy sauce
1 rounded tablespoon finely chopped
    fresh ginger
1 rounded tablespoon finely chopped
    garlic
1 rounded tablespoon finely chopped
    shallot or onion
1 level teaspoon finely chopped red chilli

To serve
225 g/8 oz tomatoes (or 1 beefsteak
    tomato), skinned, seeded and diced

Spinach and Sesame Salad

Good with grilled chicken and fish, and smoked salmon. You can obtain the ginger juice by compressing a knob of fresh ginger in a garlic press.

Bring a large pan of water to the boil. Add the spinach, bring back to the boil and cook for 1 minute. Drain into a sieve and press out as much water as possible.

Whisk together the ingredients for the dressing and mix with the spinach. Serve at room temperature, with sesame seeds scattered over.

Serves 3

450 g/1 lb spinach leaves

Dressing
1 tablespoon sesame oil
1½ tablespoons light soy sauce
2 teaspoons lemon juice
1 teaspoon ginger juice
1 level teaspoon caster sugar

To serve
toasted sesame seeds

Other Ideas

➤ Stir-fry vegetables with 1 part finely chopped fresh ginger, 1 part finely chopped garlic, and ½ part chilli.

➤ Flavour a mayonnaise with a squeeze of lime juice and ginger juice.

➤ Cook onions with fresh ginger, garlic and chilli, and add either some part-cooked potato slices and sauté together until tender, or some cooked green beans.

➤ Deep-fry fine strips of fresh ginger to use as a garnish.

➤ Make a marinade with fresh ginger, garlic, chilli, light soy sauce and groundnut oil, and steep tofu before grilling it.

➤ Stir-fry greens or oriental cabbages and season with soy sauce and ginger juice.

See also:

Oriental Stir-fried Broccoli and Cauliflower (page 37)
Oriental Late Summer Salad (page 51)
Leek Dhal with Garlic Raita (page 113)
Baked Sweet Potatoes with Ginger and Sesame Seeds (page 174)

Green Beans

There are literally hundreds of varieties of beans, with all manner of pod colour and bean colour, trailing bush beans and climbing. It is something of a mystery that we do not grow more of them. This is cultural rather than climatic. The beans we know as French beans are grown specifically for their tender pods, and it is these I shall expand upon. It may seem a little lily-livered to be so limited given the diversity of the genus, but the others remain a gardener's domain.

I can think of as many favourite ways of serving beans cold as hot, in fact more. Hot they will lend themselves to a sweet and sour tomato sauce, a few olives stirred in, or combined with broad beans in a winey butter sauce. And they are an essential addition to minestrone-style stews. When serving them cold, lightly cook or steam them, then refresh them in cold water. French beans, of all vegetables, benefit from being cooked 'al dente' (dreadful expression) – they should take 2–4 minutes depending on their thickness.

When green beans are very fine they are as much of a delicacy as asparagus – you can strew them over risottos or polenta layered with blue cheese. The larger ones can be good, but they can also be floury and stringy, and because this is unpredictable I tend to opt for the finer ones.

Beans are one of the few vegetables that refuse to succumb to the liquidizer, as anyone who has ever tried to make a purée with them can attest. You end up with a bitty mess fit for the compost heap. Cut up small is as far as they will co-operate. Terrines containing elaborate patterns of vegetables were once fashionable, but invariably were disappointing and tasteless if beans were used.

A word on buying them ready topped and tailed: you usually end up having to top and tail them all over again because they've dried out at the ends. And you will have paid extra for the privilege. Frozen beans too should be avoided, tending to be rather tasteless and flabby. Fresh has it here.

I love runner beans at the start of the season, or whenever they have been picked young: smothered in butter, occasionally with a little crispy bacon. In particular I love the recipe for them on page 95, where they are enlivened with garlic, lemon juice and coriander.

Haricot and French Beans with Champagne Butter Sauce

Vegetarians tend to miss out on *beurre blanc*, so this medley can be served as a vegetarian dish or with a poached chicken breast or monkfish on top. Do not go to the expense of fine champagne, bog-standard will do nicely, or a sparkling wine, and in case you are thinking this is a terrible waste, the flavour acquired really is distinctive.

Preheat the oven to 170°C fan oven/180°C or 350°F electric oven/ Gas 4. Place the soaked haricot beans in a casserole, cover with water and bring to the boil on the hob; skim off any white foam. Cover and cook for 1 hour in the oven, then drain.

About 15 minutes before the beans are cooked, make the sauce: place the shallots, vinegar and champagne in a small saucepan and reduce by two-thirds, then strain through a sieve back into the pan and season with salt. Whisk pieces of the butter into the reduction over a low heat, and stir in the cream; keep warm.

Bring a large pan of salted water to the boil and cook the French beans, leaving them firm to the bite. Add the warm haricot beans and French beans to the sauce, then add the spinach and leave on the heat until it wilts. At the last minute stir in the tomato and adjust the seasoning with salt and coriander.

Serves 4

---

175 g/6 oz dried haricot beans, soaked overnight
175 g/6 oz fine French beans, top and tailed
60 g/2 oz young spinach leaves
1 × 225 g/8 oz beefsteak tomato, skinned, seeded and diced
¼ teaspoon freshly ground coriander seeds

Sauce
60 g/2 oz shallots, peeled and finely chopped
1 tablespoon champagne vinegar
150 ml/5 fl oz brut champagne
sea salt
200 g/7 oz unsalted butter
2 tablespoons double cream

Polenta with Stilton and French Beans

Colston Bassett Stilton is recognized as the finest in the world: ripe and perfect for eating once it has matured to the consistency of butter right the way through, creamy in colour and marbled with a restrained number of veins the colour of green lichen, tinged with yellow and hints of blue. But once it has peaked it should be eaten within a week. So this recipe is especially apt around Christmas, when a surplus can arise. In Italy it is made with Gorgonzola.

The polenta is the consistency of porridge, layered with slivers of Stilton that melt into piquant streaks of green, spiked with a little chilli oil over the surface. The sweetness and crunch of the beans offsets it beautifully.

Place the polenta, water and salt in a saucepan and bring to the boil, stirring constantly. Then let it splutter gently for 30 minutes until thick, giving it the occasional stir, and half-covering the saucepan with a lid to stop it spitting.

While it is cooking, split the chilli and remove the seeds. Warm the oil a fraction with the chilli, and allow to marinate.

Stir the Parmesan into the cooked polenta, season with pepper, and layer with the sliced Stilton in a serving bowl, ending with a layer of polenta. Pour the chilli oil on top, discarding the chilli, and leave for 5 minutes to allow the cheese to melt.

While the cheese is melting, bring a pan of salted water to the boil and top and tail the beans: boil them for about 3 minutes, leaving them firm to the bite. Drain, and serve with the polenta.

Photograph between pages 80 and 81.

Serves 4

225 g/8 oz coarse polenta
1.2 litres/2 pints water
1 level teaspoon sea salt
1 fresh red chilli
2 tablespoons extra virgin olive oil
2 heaped tablespoons freshly grated
　Parmesan
freshly ground black pepper
175 g/6 oz Stilton, excluding rind, sliced
225 g/8 oz fine French beans

Lebanese Runner Beans

This is delicious eaten with feta cheese and also, I am told, with grilled lamb chops. It is adapted from a recipe for broad beans in oil, in Nada Saleh's wonderful book on Lebanese cooking *Fragrance of the Earth*. You will need a big bunch of coriander.

Top and tail the beans, remove the strings at the side with a potato peeler, and cut diagonally into 2.5 cm/1 inch lengths. Heat the oil in a medium-sized pan over a moderate heat and cook the onions, stirring, until pale and translucent. Add the beans, reduce the heat, cover the pan and let them sweat in their own juices for 8 minutes.

Add the garlic, coriander and flour to the pan, then add the cinnamon, allspice, salt and pepper, and the water. Bring to a boil, cover, and simmer over a low heat for 15 minutes until tender. Remove from the heat, stir in the lemon juice, and adjust the salt as necessary. Serve warm or at room temperature.

Serves 4

500 g/1 lb 2 oz runner beans
2 tablespoons extra virgin olive oil
2 onions, peeled and chopped
3–4 large garlic cloves, peeled and crushed
70 g/2½ oz coriander sprigs, chopped
1 teaspoon flour
¼ teaspoon cinnamon
pinch of allspice
1 teaspoon sea salt
¼ teaspoon freshly ground black pepper
150 ml/5 fl oz water
2 tablespoons lemon juice

Other Ideas

➤ Along with carrots, cooked green beans are one of the best vegetables for dunking into dips.

➤ Make a vegetarian aïoli with a selection of vegetables, raw and cooked: radishes, fennel, green beans, butter beans. Include some quail's eggs and black olives, and serve with a large bowl of garlic mayonnaise, made by adding a garlic clove, peeled, finely chopped and crushed to a paste with a sprinkling of salt, to the finished mayonnaise.

➤ Make a salad with cooked green beans, walnuts, pears and a walnut dressing.

➤ An oriental sesame dressing goes well with cooked green beans: make it with 3 tablespoons of sesame seeds ground in an electric grinder, mixed with 2 tablespoons of ketjap manis (an Indonesian aromatic sweet sauce similar to Chinese sweet soy sauce, or use dark soy sauce sweetened with a little sugar), 2 tablespoons of sake and 2 tablespoons of vegetable stock or water.

➤ Dress cooked green beans and pulses with balsamic vinegar, mustard, olive oil and chopped shallots.

➤ Make a base of sweated onions and spices such as cumin, coriander and ground ginger, then add beans and a little chopped tomato and 'smother' them on a low heat in a covered pan until they are tender.

See also:

Beetroot, French Bean and Hazelnut Salad with Toasted Goat's Cheese (page 27)
Three Bean Salad Served Warm with Balsamic Vinaigrette (page 31)
Oriental Late Summer Salad (page 51)

Horseradish

In Russia, when things aren't going too well, they are described as 'horseradishy' – *khrenovo*. The plant probably originated in southern Russia and the Eastern Ukraine, and now grows wild throughout Great Britain. Having persuaded my mother-in-law to plant a single horseradish plant in her vegetable garden, she did not subsequently thank me. Once present, it becomes virtually impossible to remove, spreading with triffid-like tendencies. It has large, coarse leaves and a very deep, forked root, which is gnarled and brown, with coarse fibres.

Horseradish belongs to the same botanical family as radishes. Wasabi is not in fact related, even though it is called Japanese horseradish. Freshly grated horseradish is fabuously pungent and hits the top of your palate. The closest association to this pungency is mustard: it is the volatile oils that provide the heat. Like mustard, it has an affinity with ham, beef, tongue and so forth, and is often served with oily fish like mackerel and smoked salmon. More alarmingly, it was once used as a poultice to relieve neuralgia, and an infusion in vinegar was supposed to clear freckles.

If novices are given tests of strength, then as a fledgling chef mine was grating a large pile of horseradish by hand. First it needs peeling, which is simple enough with a potato peeler, but from there on as you grate it the air is filled with a pungent, slightly sweet and earthy aroma, and at the same time with lethal fumes which sting your eyes. The tears caused by onions seem trivial compared to those created by grating horseradish.

The greatest sins against this root are the heavily vinegared ready-made relishes. As a seasoning it is very under-used, though all manner of partners spring to mind: cheese, beetroot, celeriac, asparagus and crab, sashimi of tuna, scallops or salmon. I ate a memorable salad at the Brackenbury restaurant in Shepherd's Bush, a mixture of different salad leaves with lots of different mustards. On top were thin slices of pink pigeon breast, and surrounding it were croûtons thickly spread with a really pungent, creamy horseradish sauce.

Preparation

There is nothing in the texture of horseradish to recommend eating it as a vegetable – it is purely a flavouring agent. It provides its own burst of heat, yet strangely demands that black pepper is present. Lemon juice and Dijon mustard also go well with it.

Once grated, it quickly loses its pungency and discolours. But you can mix it with some sour or double cream and deep-freeze it. I am not one to recommend freezers, but this does make sense considering the difficulties of grating it. If you have a food processor, use the Parmesan grating attachment rather than doing it by hand.

Puff Pastry Tart with Asparagus and Horseradish

Elegant and easy to make are two selling points here: asparagus spears lie side by side on top of a puff pastry base, with a cream patched with gold spread over the surface.

Preheat the oven to 190°C fan oven/200°C or 400°F electric oven/ Gas 6.

Bring a large pan of salted water to the boil. Trim the asparagus where it begins to become woody and peel the spears to within 2.5 cm/1 inch of the tip. Add to the pan, bring back to the boil and cook for 4 minutes. Drain into a sink of cold water. Remove and dry on a tea-towel.

Roll the pastry 0.25 cm/⅛ inch thick into a rectangle 41 × 20.5 cm/ 16 × 8 inches and trim to neaten the edges – make sure you have a baking sheet large enough, otherwise adjust the dimensions accordingly. Lay the pastry on the baking sheet, and lay the asparagus in rows of single spears, so that there is a pastry surround of 2.5 cm/1 inch. Beat the egg yolks and paint the pastry border. Bake the tart for 15 minutes.

Blend the crème fraîche, horseradish, Parmesan, beaten egg yolks and seasoning together in a bowl. Spoon this cream over the asparagus and bake for another 15 minutes until golden on the top. Serve 5 minutes out of the oven, though it is also excellent cold.

Serves 4

450 g/1 lb finger-thick asparagus spears
250 g/9 oz ready-made puff pastry
2 medium egg yolks
150 ml/5 fl oz crème fraîche
2 heaped teaspoons grated horseradish
2 tablespoons freshly grated Parmesan
sea salt and freshly ground black pepper

Aubergine Purée

Serve this with lengths of fried courgette, or with melba toast and olive oil, crostini, or warm pitta bread for dunking. It would make a good accompaniment to chargrilled squid or smoked fish.

Preheat the oven to 200°C fan oven/220°C or 425°F electric oven/ Gas 7. Prick the aubergines and bake for 25 minutes until the skin is wrinkled and darker. While they are cooking, soak the bread in water for 5 minutes, then squeeze out the water, though not too dry. Place in a food processor with the garlic, vinegar and horseradish and process to a smooth cream. With the motor running, add the olive oil.

Skin the aubergines and slice the cooked flesh thickly. Place in a sieve and press out as much of their juice as possible. Add the flesh to the bread mixture in the food processor and purée together, adding seasoning. Serve with a swirl of olive oil poured over.

Serves 4

1 kg/2 lb 4 oz aubergines (3 large ones)
4 slices day-old white bread, crusts removed
1 garlic clove, peeled and coarsely chopped
1 tablespoon red wine vinegar
1 level tablespoon freshly grated horseradish
5 tablespoons extra virgin olive oil
sea salt and freshly ground black pepper

To serve
extra virgin olive oil

Other Ideas

➤ Make a Welsh rarebit in the usual way with a mature, farmhouse Cheddar, and add a teaspoon of horseradish to the blend.

➤ Make a salad of warm new potatoes and cresses and drizzle over a horse-radish cream.

➤ Make a beetroot and sorrel soup by adding finely shredded sorrel to the hot soup at the very end and cooking until it turns a dull green. Serve the soup with a spoon of horseradish sour cream in the centre.

➤ Serve poached wild salmon with a horseradish sauce.

➤ Bake mackerel with a topping of breadcrumbs, herbs and horseradish.

➤ Make a warm salad with a mixture of leaves and wild mushrooms, and accompany with croûtons spread with horseradish cream.

Jerusalem Artichokes

To complicate matters straight off, these are native to North America – Jerusalem, the place, doesn't really come into it. It is most likely that the name Jerusalem is a derived from 'girasol', meaning sunflower. Nor are they connected to globe artichokes, except maybe distantly in terms of flavour.

Crisp ivory flesh beneath a buff-coloured skin with occasional purplish tinges, these roots have a delicious nutty flavour and are surprisingly aromatic. If their grip on our culinary imagination is not as firm as it could be, I suspect this is because of their well-documented side-effects.

They are a wintertime vegetable, and they fit very naturally into the whole chilly scene of roasts, chestnuts, wild mushrooms and braises. I think my favourite way of cooking them is to 'stove' them (see the recipe below), whereby they emerge wonderfully golden, crisp and chewy on the outside, and melting within. Because of their tendency to collapse when boiled, they also make very good purées and cream soups. And when not overcooked they make a delicious salad, especially dressed with a hazelnut vinaigrette.

Preparation

Choose artichokes that are firm; they go soft as they are getting old. When peeling them, (to prevent them from discolouring), reserve them in a bowl of water acidulated with lemon juice or vinegar.

In old cookery books there is a lot of talk about the difficulty of peeling these knobbly tubers. But modern varieties seem to have the knobbly bits bred out of them and are no harder to peel than a potato. So no moaning on this score, and if you do happen to acquire a good old-fashioned batch you can always cook them in their skins and scrape out the cooked inside.

Cooking

To cook Jerusalem artichokes, bring a pan of water to the boil, acidulate it with lemon juice or vinegar, then boil them until tender. The point at which they are cooked must be carefully gauged, as they very quickly progress from cooked to collapsing, at which point all they will be good for is a purée or a soup.

Jerusalem Artichoke and Stilton Soufflé

When I mentioned soufflé to Patrice de Villier, the photographer at the *Independent*, she said, 'Well, that's one to avoid.' Don't worry – this is the 'faux' version; it began life as pancakes and ended up half-way between a soufflé and a batter pudding, and as long as you can whisk an egg white it is foolproof. The result is exquisitely tender, and the Stilton is added in chunks which melt down as it cooks.

Bring a pan of water to the boil and acidulate it with vinegar. Peel the artichokes and boil them for 10–15 minutes until tender. Drain them and place in a liquidizer with the cream, flour, whole eggs, butter and seasoning. Whizz to a purée.

Butter an 18 cm/7 inch soufflé dish and dust with breadcrumbs. You can prepare the soufflé to this point in advance.

Preheat the oven to 200°C fan oven/220°C or 425°F electric oven/ Gas 7. Pour the batter into a large bowl. Whisk the egg whites in a separate bowl until they are stiff, and fold them in 2 batches into the batter. Fold in the diced Stilton and pour into the prepared mould. Allow plenty of headroom and bake for 25–30 minutes in total, turning the oven down to 160°C fan oven/170°C or 325°F electric oven/Gas 3 after 5 minutes. Serve immediately – I like it runny in the centre, so don't worry if you cut into it and find this is the case.

Serves 4

white wine vinegar for acidulating water
450 g/1 lb Jerusalem artichokes
125 ml/4 fl oz double cream
1 heaped tablespoon plain flour
2 medium eggs, plus 2 egg whites
25 g/1 oz unsalted butter, melted
sea salt, freshly ground black pepper and
    grated nutmeg
110 g/4 oz Stilton, diced

For mould
unsalted butter
breadcrumbs

Stoved Jerusalem Artichokes with Provençal Herbs

Peel the artichokes; if there is going to be any delay in cooking them, reserve them in a bowl of water acidulated with white wine vinegar or a little lemon juice. Arrange all the ingredients in a saucepan so that the artichokes are in a single layer. Put the pan over a high heat until the oil is sizzling, then cover, turn the heat down low and cook for 10 minutes, turning them half-way through.

Uncover the pan, turn up the heat and cook for another 10 minutes, until the artichokes and garlic cloves are golden on the outside and tender inside – again turn them half-way through. You can extract the soft inside of the garlic cloves to eat with the artichokes.

Serves 4

700 g/1 lb 9 oz Jerusalem artichokes
12 garlic cloves, peeled
4 bay leaves
8 sprigs of thyme
4 sprigs of rosemary
5 tablespoons extra virgin olive oil
sea salt and freshly ground black pepper

Salad of Jerusalem Artichokes, Rocket and Hazelnuts

Put a large pan of water on to boil, acidulate it with a slug of vinegar, and acidulate a bowl of water for the artichokes. Peel the artichokes and reserve in the bowl of water, then boil them for 8–10 minutes until they are tender and a knife can be inserted with ease. Drain into a sieve and allow to cool.

To make the dressing, whisk the vinegar with the mustard and seasoning. Add the oils.

To serve the salad, slice the artichokes and place in a large bowl. Toss them with the dressing, add the hazelnuts, then toss in the rocket and serve straight away.

Serves 4

white wine vinegar
700 g/1 lb 9 oz Jerusalem
    artichokes
40 g/1½ oz toasted chopped
    hazelnuts
80 g/3 oz rocket

Dressing
1 tablespoon red wine vinegar
¾ teaspoon Dijon mustard
sea salt and freshly ground black pepper
2 tablespoons groundnut oil
4 tablespoons hazelnut or walnut oil

Roasted Root Vegetables with Rocket Pesto (page 130)

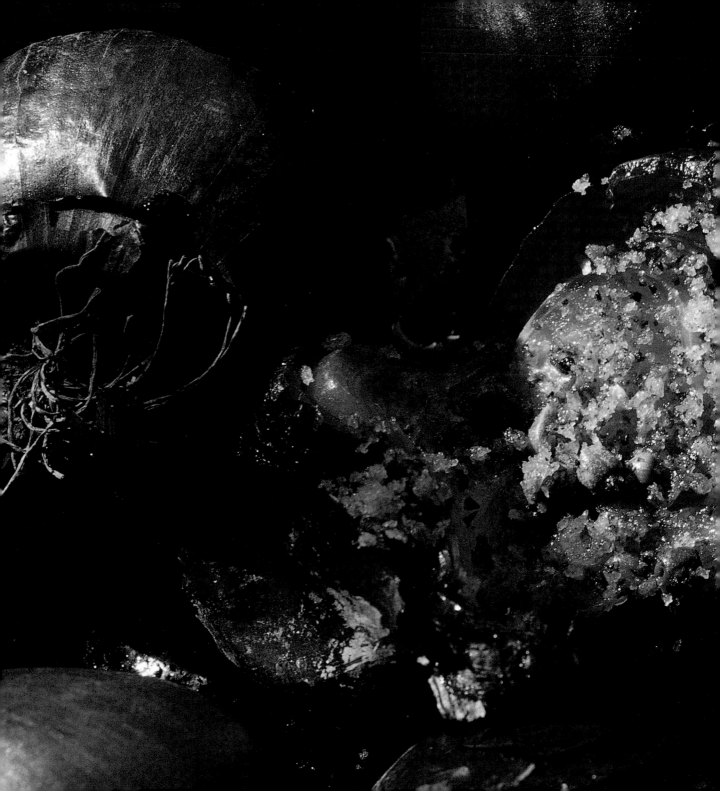

Bruschetta with Raclette and an Onion Salad (page 126)

Baked Red Onions with Sicilian Crumbs (page 125)

Other Ideas

➤ Make a Jerusalem artichoke purée and add a spoonful of hollandaise or béchamel sauce for a really smooth, rich finish.

➤ Dress cooked and sliced Jerusalem artichokes and peeled prawns with lemon juice and olive oil, and scatter over lots of snipped chives.

➤ Make a creamed artichoke soup and flavour it with a large pinch of curry spices, ideally freshly ground.

➤ Jerusalem artichokes make a wonderfully creamy gratin, sliced and arranged in a shallow ovenproof dish with double cream, then baked. You could add some whole cloves of garlic between the layers.

➤ They make a delicious mousse with a layer of mushroom duxelles – finely minced and fried – lining the mould.

➤ Make a Jerusalem artichoke and hazelnut salad with boiled and sliced artichokes, roasted and chopped hazelnuts, and a little tarragon in the dressing.

See also:

Michel Guérard's Carrot Flan – Jerusalem Artichoke Purée (page 48)
Truffled Artichokes and New Potatoes (page 146)

Petits Pois à la Française (page 135)

Kohlrabi

Kohlrabi has the look of a turnip having a bad hair day. Round and usually a little smaller than a tennis ball, its skin has a satin-smooth finish, in a shade of eau-de-nil or lascivious purple. From there on its leaves jut out at right angles to the bulb, giving it the appearance of something from outer space, a mixture of beauty and beast.

When you meet this vegetable for the first time, it is perfectly normal to be confounded – 'Any recipes for kohlrabi?' is a question I have been asked on more than one occasion by those in receipt of organic boxes, who do not get any choice over what they are getting. And the answer is a few, but to be honest not that many. Kohlrabi has been grown on these shores for several hundreds of years and we're still treating it like a stranger. We like it, but we don't love it.

A member of the cabbage family, the stem remains short and swells. As to taste, I would describe it as a cross between a radish and a turnip, with hints of rocket thrown in. Not surprisingly it is sometimes called turnip-rooted cabbage.

Most recipes that are good for turnip are good for kohlrabi – and it has the added advantage of being good to eat raw. I have a stated preference for the green variety; I find the purple ones rather tough.

Preparation

To prepare kohlrabi, it needs to be peeled. Try to find ones no larger than a tennis ball. The area immediately below the skin can be fibrous, so peel it amply. When serving it in salads be sure to slice it wafer thin – it actually looks quite pretty like this.

Creamed Kohlrabi with Chervil

Either serve this as a side dish, or, even better, add some beaten eggs at the very end and stir until they begin to scramble, stopping short of firm while they are still nicely 'baveuse', and eat on toast.

Cut the skin off the kohlrabi, halve, and slice transparently thin. Melt the butter in a frying pan and sweat the kohlrabi slices for 10 minutes over a medium heat until they are translucent and beginning to colour. Add the garlic and season, then add the cream and cook until this thickens. Stir in the chervil and serve straight away.

Serves 4

700 g/1 lb 9 oz green kohlrabi
25 g/1 oz unsalted butter
1 garlic clove, peeled and finely chopped
sea salt and freshly ground black pepper
150 ml/5 fl oz double cream
2 heaped tablespoons coarsely chopped chervil

Sesame Coleslaw

This is a variation on the theme of coleslaw; only better than – it makes a nice change from the cabbagey versions.

Cut the skin off the kohlrabi and grate it by hand. Place in a tea-towel and squeeze out most of the liquid.

Make a mayonnaise by whisking the egg yolk with the mustard in a bowl, and gradually whisking in the oil in a thin stream until very thick. Blend in the soy sauce, sesame oil and lemon or lime juice.

Combine the grated kohlrabi, shallot or onion and mayonnaise and place in a shallow dish. Toast the sesame seeds in a dry frying pan until they start to colour, and allow to cool. Serve the coleslaw scattered with the sesame seeds.

Serves 4

600 g/1 lb 4 oz kohlrabi
1 egg yolk (size 2)
¾ teaspoon grainy mustard
200 ml/7 fl oz groundnut oil
1 teaspoon light soy sauce
1 teaspoon sesame oil
squeeze of lemon or lime juice
1 heaped teaspoon grated shallot or onion
1 heaped teaspoon sesame seeds

Other Ideas

➤ Sauté fine slices of kohlrabi and caramelize with a pinch of sugar.

➤ Make a smooth soup by puréeing kohlrabi in a liquidizer, and serve with a spoon of curry cream in the centre: fry a little curry powder in butter for a few seconds only, then add sour cream and a squeeze of lemon juice.

➤ Use kohlrabi grated in salads. The trick when dressing it with mayonnaise is to squeeze out the liquid first in a tea-towel, otherwise the whole thing goes rather watery.

➤ Use kohlrabi as one of the components in a vegetable stew or minestrone, and in tagines.

➤ Make a salad of finely sliced kohlrabi, cubes of blue cheese, walnuts, chives and a dressing of red wine vinegar and olive oil.

➤ Cut up the kohlrabi and roast them with olive oil or clarified butter. Or roast a mélange of vegetables as on page 130 and serve with a pesto or chopped herbs.

➤ Braise small kohlrabi with butter, seasoning, sugar and a little stock until they are sweet and tender.

➤ Make a gratin of finely sliced kohlrabi, with lots of double cream and seasoning. You could also add Fontina cheese between the layers.

Leeks

Any vegetable that forms the focus of a competition has a headstart in image. Northumbrian leek shows have always been a point of fascination for me – great big brutes that are totally inedible are put on display, assuming, that is, that they have escaped sabotage by a close competitor: intrigue and mystery at the potting shed, as far as I can gather, after the pubs have closed.

Suffice to say that leeks can be bred up to gargantuan dimensions; as with other vegetables, however, little is to be gained beyond a certain size as the texture coarsens – and in the case of leeks a woody heart develops. Baby leeks, though, are one of the few infant vegetables worth cooking. There is no need to remove tough outer layers, and they are compact, rarely having trapped any grit between their layers. They are heavenly braised with a little white wine, butter and thyme sprigs until they are sweet and tender, tasting just mildly of onions.

Leeks are multi-talented: apart from starring in one of the sexiest cold soups ever, vichyssoise, the texture of liquid velvet – at its most glorious with a spoon of caviar in the centre – you can roast them, grill them, barbecue, braise or sauté them.

Large leeks divide into dark green and white, a division of status not unlike that of the crab: the dark upper shoots tend to land in the stockpot. I have learnt, though, to ignore recipes that demand white of leek only, and to extend this brief to white and pale green, of which there is quite a lot on a leek.

I often buy ready trimmed leeks because you get a better idea of how much there is to cook with. It can be frustrating to arrive home and trim up your large bag of leeks only to find that there isn't enough for the recipe. This is quite genuinely a problem, because different varieties will yield varying amounts of pale green and white parts.

Béchamel would not be my first choice of treatment; it is too bland. Leeks need a certain piquancy, be it citrus juice or wine, some olives or mustard, thyme when braising, chopped parsley or coriander in a salad.

Preparation

If you are cleaning leeks in order to cook them whole, slit them down to the point where the white of leek begins, and fan out the layers under a tap. This isn't always necessary; you can usually see dark shadows where dirt has been trapped. As a precaution you can give them a jolly good soak for 15 minutes.

Cooking

If the leeks are old, I prefer to boil rather than to steam them. If you do happen to have missed a pocket of dirt it stands some chance of coming out in the wash, while if you steam them it's stuck. With baby leeks this isn't so important.

Baby leeks can be griddled from raw, large specimens need a few minutes' boiling first. I also like roasting leeks, in the same way the Spanish cook spring onions over an open fire and then extract the centre for dipping into a romesco sauce – the centre of a roasted leek will be especially sweet and concentrated in flavour.

Roasted Leeks Vinaigrette

A chic little salad that fares well left overnight. For non-vegetarian picnics in the past I have wrapped the leeks up in slices of air-dried ham, such as Parma, Bayonne or serrano. You would need 12 slices for this – and omit the egg.

Preheat the oven to 180°C fan oven/190°C or 375°F electric oven/ Gas 5. Remove the outer layer of the leeks, or more if you can see dirt trapped. Place in a baking dish, pour over 3 tablespoons of the oil, the wine and seasoning and bake for 50 minutes. Once cool enough to handle, slit the leeks to remove the cooked centre and discard the dried outer layer. Cut the leeks lengthwise into thin 5 cm/2 inch strips.

Blend the vinegar with the mustard and seasoning and add the remaining oil and the roasting juices. Pour the dressing over the leeks. Cover and chill until required – the salad will improve overnight.

To serve, bring back to room temperature. Peel the eggs and discard one of the whites. Finely chop the yolks and the remaining white and scatter over the salad.

Serves 4

800 g/1¾ lb leeks, trimmed weight
5 tablespoons extra virgin olive oil
2 tablespoons white wine
sea salt and freshly ground black pepper
2 teaspoons red wine vinegar
½ teaspoon Dijon mustard
2 eggs, boiled for 10 minutes

Leek and Smoked Cheddar Tart

If you are a vegetarian who craves smoky bacon sarnies, this tart is bound to come as a nostalgic reminder. I have suggested smoked Cheddar, but Spanish Idiazabal, a Basque sheep's milk cheese traditionally made on small farms and hung up in chimneys, a smoked Lancashire or other sheep's milk cheese could also be used.

To prepare the pastry, mix together the egg yolk, sugar, salt and water. Combine the flour and butter in a food processor until the mixture resembles fine crumbs. Bring the dough together with the egg and water solution and knead it for a few minutes with a sprinkling of flour, then wrap it in clingfilm and rest it in the fridge for 45 minutes.

Heat the oven to 200°C fan oven/220°C or 425°F electric oven/ Gas 7. Butter and flour a shallow 23 cm/9 inch tart case with a removable base. Lightly flour a work surface, knead the pastry until it softens, then roll it 0.25 cm/⅛ inch thick and line the case. Trim it, allowing 0.25 cm/⅛ inch above the top of the rim for shrinkage. Line the case with foil and baking beans and cook for 15 minutes. Remove the foil and beans and cook for another 7–10 minutes until starting to colour.

While preparing the pastry, slice the leeks thinly. Melt the butter in a frying pan, add the leeks, thyme and seasoning and sweat for 5 minutes. Cover with a lid and sweat over a low heat for a further 5 minutes, stirring once. Whisk the cream, milk and egg together and season. Slice the cheese into long thin strips.

Place the leeks and cheese in the bottom of the tart case, place in the oven, pour the custard into the case and scatter over the chives. Bake for 15 minutes until patched with gold on the surface. Serve hot or at room temperature, but avoid chilling.

Serves 4

250 g/9 oz leeks (trimmed weight)
25 g/1 oz unsalted butter
1 teaspoon thyme leaves
sea salt and freshly ground black pepper
125 ml/4 fl oz double cream
125 ml/4 fl oz milk
1 medium egg
125 g/4½ oz smoked Cheddar
1 heaped tablespoon snipped chives

Pastry
1 medium egg yolk
½ teaspoon caster sugar
½ teaspoon sea salt
65 ml/2½ fl oz water
250 g/9 oz plain flour, sifted
70 g/2½ oz unsalted butter, diced

Leek Dhal with Garlic Raita

I can think of several young children who regard dhal as a 'best favourite' – you can substitute plain Greek yoghurt for the raita. Added to this, it is inexpensive and nutritious, it can be made up by the large saucepanful, and it reheats well. Serve with warm pitta bread.

Heat the oven to 180°C fan oven/190°C or 375°F electric oven/ Gas 5. Slice the top off the head of garlic, wrap it in foil and roast for 20–30 minutes; allow to cool.

While the garlic is cooking, make the dhal. Heat the butter in a large saucepan, add the garlic, ginger and sliced leeks and sweat over a low heat for several minutes without colouring. Add the lentils, tomato, chillies, spices, salt and 1.2 litres/2 pints of water, bring to the boil, skim any surface foam and simmer for 30–40 minutes, stirring occasionally. Add the lemon juice or Seville orange juice, discard the chillies and adjust the salt.

To finish making the raita, squeeze the cooked inside of the garlic into a bowl, mash it with the crème fraîche and Greek yoghurt and season with salt.

Serve the dhal hot, with a dollop of raita and plenty of chopped coriander scattered over.

Serves 3

Dhal
40 g/1½ oz unsalted butter
2 garlic cloves, peeled and minced
1 heaped teaspoon finely minced fresh ginger
350 g/12 oz leeks (trimmed weight), sliced
250 g/9 oz red lentils, rinsed
1 beefsteak tomato (225 g/8 oz), skinned and chopped
2 red chillies
1 heaped teaspoon cumin, freshly ground
1 heaped teaspoon coriander, freshly ground
¼ teaspoon turmeric
1 heaped teaspoon sea salt
1 tablespoon lemon juice or Seville orange juice

Raita
1 large head of garlic
2 tablespoons crème fraîche
3 heaped tablespoons Greek yoghurt

To serve
chopped coriander

Leeks in White Wine

Leeks are one of the vegetables I often buy as a standby without really knowing in what guise they will end up. And the recipe that I turn to again and again is one that I included in my first book, *A Feast of Flavours*. As a fast recipe I don't think it can be beaten, so here it is once more. The original can be found in Jane Grigson's *Vegetable Book*.

Trim the root off each leek and cut off the dark green shoots. Remove the outer layer of leaves and rinse the surface. Cut the leeks into slices 0.5 cm/¼ inch thick and rinse well in a sieve.

Place all the ingredients in a saucepan. Bring the liquid to the boil, cover the pan, and cook over a low heat for 25–30 minutes. Remove the lid. The leeks should be coated in a butter sauce, but if there is liquid remaining, turn up the heat and continue cooking until it has all but evaporated.

Serves 4

700 g/1 lb 9 oz leeks
50 g/2 oz unsalted butter
150 ml/5 fl oz dry white wine
sea salt and freshly ground black pepper

Other Ideas

➤ Braise leeks until they are tender with cooked flageolet or haricot beans, thyme, wine, butter, soaked dried porcini and their juices. Scatter over fried breadcrumbs at the end.

➤ Make a salad of steamed or boiled young leeks and avocado, and dress with balsamic or red wine vinegar laced with grainy mustard, and extra virgin olive oil. You could toss in a few rocket or mâche leaves, and top with a slice of creamy blue cheese or ricotta.

➤ Serve leeks that have been griddled on a ridged grill with shavings of Parmesan and more olive oil.

➤ Make a leek and potato pizza using cooked baby leeks — shave over black truffles for a treat.

➤ Leeks melt down to an unctuous consistency in a risotto.

➤ For a variation on the classic French flamiche, quiche aux poireaux: pre-bake a puff pastry case and sweat leeks with garlic, thyme, olive oil and butter. Make a custard with cream, egg yolks and a little egg, and pour into the case on top of the chopped leeks. Smother with lots of grated Gruyère and bake until golden.

➤ Being a classic winter vegetable, make a pot-au-feu by braising carrots, turnips, leeks, celeriac, parsnips, wild mushrooms and herbs such as bay, parsley and thyme, with vegetable stock, white wine and olive oil — and serve with a red pepper and chilli mayonnaise.

See also:

Petits Pois à la Française (page 135)

Mushrooms

As a food writer I did a maiden voyage to Northern Italy, to the mushroom market in Trento. This is a fungiphile's dream: something like 200 varieties of wild mushroom pass through the stalls during the course of the year, all picked locally. The vetting of them is professionally handled by state-trained inspectors; if you happen to have been foraging, you can take your booty to be checked by them early in the morning.

Within the market stalls the more precious of the mushrooms are sold separately, but most of the varieties are bundled together and sold as mixed mushrooms. I confess I am not that fond of the mixed selection – there is a pecking order with mushrooms, and I have detailed below those that I feel are really worth pursuing or paying for. The precise pecking order is largely a matter of personal taste; ask a Frenchman and he'll tell you girolles rule, ask an Italian and he'll say it's porcini.

Wild mushrooms have become the signature luxury of vegetarians. I can almost guarantee that if I order the vegetarian special in a restaurant during the autumn it will have its requisite portion of chanterelles and girolles, or porcini.

There is no denying that wild mushrooms fetch a premium, the consolation being that a little goes a long way. Just a few will spread their heady fragrance in a recipe: a pasta sauce, a risotto, an omelette. And, of course, there is always the option of dried wild mushrooms. Porcini dry especially well; their flavour concentrates in the process. I remember being fascinated by the dried porcini for sale in Italy, which were sometimes 15 cm/6 inches in diameter. Over here we tend to find more modest slices. The important thing is that they shouldn't be broken. Other good dried mushrooms are morels, fiercely expensive but excellent, and shiitake.

I know it is easy enough to go out and pick your own wild mushrooms, but I do not advise it. I say this after discovering how rigorously trained the inspectors are in Northern Italy. And I'm afraid they do have fatalities among the public each year because people have foraged without really knowing enough about their findings. Luckily the shops are full of wild mushrooms, and while they don't come free you are paying for peace of mind and safety. Leave the picking to the Italians.

As to cultivated mushrooms, shiitake have a distinctive flavour and texture and these will serve as a poor man's wild mushroom when you want something more exciting than the standard cultivated types, and less expensive than the wild ones. Quite often I use these mixed in with wild.

Oyster mushrooms are different again, but I am not overly fond of these – I do not think they have much in the way of flavour or texture to recommend them. All the others can be safely bunched together in terms of flavour, from the diminutive button mushrooms through to the large flat caps. If anything it is their size that demands they receive different treatment when being cooked: the caps are best stuffed and grilled, while button mushrooms can be used à la grècque. The big ones also turn a muddy colour when sautéed, while the button ones remain pristine, which is something to be taken into account if you are mixing them in with another food that you do not want dyed.

Top wild mushrooms

There are so many common names for the same mushroom that the only reliable reference is the Latin name:

Girolle (*Cantharellus cibarius*) – highly prized, golden and apricot-scented, this mushroom retains its texture when cooked.

Chanterelle (*Cantharellus tubaeformis*) – these have spindly yellow stems and brown caps, and cook to a soft brown mass.

Horn of Plenty (*Craterellus cornucopioides*) – trumpet-shaped, grey-black and hollow, these are especially good with fish.

Penny Bun, Cep or Porcini (*Boletus edulis*) – delectable

plump mushrooms that range hugely in size, with distinctive cream stems and rounded caps. The small ones are good eaten raw.

Morel (*Morchella esculenta*) – a springtime mushroom, one of the most prized, these have a honeycombed head and a hollow stalk.

Hedgehog fungus (*Hydnum repandum*) – these have delicate spines beneath the cap, they are firm and scented and make a good substitute for girolles.

Preparing dried wild mushrooms

One joy of these is the speed with which they are brought back to life: cover with boiling water in a bowl and leave to soak for 15 minutes, then remove the mushrooms and chop if the recipe requires it. Reserve the soaking liquor for use as stock, either in the recipe or in some other dish; it can be frozen. Check before you use it that no grit has collected in the bottom of the bowl; if it has, decant the liquid, discarding the last little gritty bit, as you would mussel juices.

Cooking wild mushrooms

The only wild mushrooms I like to eat raw are very small porcini; these are delicious finely sliced in a salad.

As regards the others, they should be first sautéed. Mushrooms contain varying quantities of water – some will cook and remain dry, others reduce to a soggy mess. So you should proceed as follows: pick over your wild mushrooms and cut off any bits that are slimy or messy. If the mushrooms are large, slice them. You can fry the mushrooms in a mixture of olive oil and butter, or in clarified butter (as well as plain olive oil), the point being that it should become very hot so as to sear the mushrooms. If it is not hot enough they tend to weep in the process of cooking. Season them at the end if you want them to remain dry, because salt will draw out their juices.

If the mushrooms do give out a lot of liquid and you don't want this, either continue to cook until it evaporates, or heat some more oil and fry the mushrooms a second time.

Standard cultivated mushrooms can be cooked in the same fashion; they do not tend to hold as much water as wild ones.

Wild Mushroom Cassoulet

This is a hearty one-pot dish which I first made in the Camargue with a selection of local mushrooms; more recently I have made it with girolles, which are equally wonderful. The aubergine provides a luscious texture, and the whole thing is scented with Provençal herbs and topped with crisp breadcrumbs.

Preheat the oven to 180°C fan oven/190°C or 375°F electric oven/ Gas 5.

To skin the tomatoes, bring a pan of water to the boil, remove a small cone from the top of each one to remove the core, then immerse them in the boiling water for 20 seconds. Plunge the tomatoes into cold water, slip off the skins and coarsely chop the flesh.

Heat 2 tablespoons of oil in a frying pan and when it is very hot throw in the aubergine and cook, stirring, until golden. Pick over and slice the mushrooms if large. Remove the aubergine and heat the remaining oil and the butter in the frying pan, add the mushrooms and cook until starting to colour. Season towards the end – if the juices flow this is fine.

Combine the beans, aubergine, mushrooms, garlic and herbs in a gratin or other shallow ovenproof dish, and season. Arrange the tomatoes on top, pour over the wine, and bake for 30 minutes. Stir the mixture, then scatter over the breadcrumbs and return to the oven for 25–30 minutes until golden and crisp.

Serves 4

---

700 g/1 lb 9 oz beefsteak tomatoes
4 tablespoons extra virgin olive oil
1 large aubergine, cut into 1 cm/½ inch
    cubes
300 g/10½ oz wild mushrooms
15 g/½ oz unsalted butter
sea salt and freshly ground black pepper
1 × 400 g/14 oz tin haricot or flageolet
    beans
7 garlic cloves, peeled
2 sprigs of rosemary
2 bay leaves
3 sprigs of thyme
125 ml/4 fl oz white wine
100 g/3½ oz breadcrumbs mixed with
    3 tablespoons extra virgin olive oil

Aubergines with a Porcini Crust

Serve these with a small green salad as a starter or light lunch. For a main course, bake the aubergine on top of a fresh tomato sauce: sweat some garlic and shallot in olive oil, add about 700 g/1 lb 9 oz of tomatoes, peeled, seeded and diced, cook until this softens, then add 100 ml/ 3½ fl oz of passata and place the stuffed slices on top.

Quinoa is a tiny, bead-shaped grain that was a staple of the ancient Incas. It is considered a complete protein because it contains all eight essential amino acids, which makes it very valuable for vegetarians.

Preheat the oven to 200°C fan oven/220°C or 425°F electric oven/ Gas 7. Slice the aubergines into 2.5 cm/1 inch rounds, brush generously with olive oil and season. Lay out on a baking tray and bake for 25 minutes.

Bring a small pan of salted water to the boil and cook the quinoa for 15 minutes: drain, rinse under the cold tap and reserve. Soak the porcini in boiling water for 15 minutes, then drain, reserving the liquor for some other use, and coarsely chop the mushrooms. Blend all the ingredients for the crust to a paste in a food processor and season. Spread a thin layer on to each round of cooked aubergine. Bake the aubergine slices for 25 minutes, until lightly golden on the surface. Serve hot or cold, with extra olive oil splashed over.

Serves 4

2 aubergines
extra virgin olive oil
sea salt and freshly ground black pepper

Crust
60 g/2 oz quinoa
15 g/½ oz dried porcini
1 teaspoon thyme leaves
3 tablespoons finely chopped flat-leaved parsley
1 level dessertspoon chopped basil
1 small garlic clove, peeled and finely chopped
80 g/3 oz grated Gruyère
60 g/2 oz unsalted butter
1 teaspoon grainy mustard

Caramelized Red Onion, Girolles and Blue Cheese Pizza

I do recommend pizza crispers: pans with a slotted base which assist in browning the underneath, hence overcoming the problem of domestic ovens not being as hot as a proper bread oven. If you have a very hot oven, you should be able to reduce this cooking time – heat it on its highest setting.

If using fresh yeast, dissolve it in a little of the water, adding the sugar, and leave it for 10 minutes until a froth appears on the surface. Add this to the dry ingredients and proceed as if using dried yeast.

Place all the dry ingredients in a bowl, add the olive oil and gradually add the water, bringing the dough together with your hand. The amount of water is for guidance only. If you add too much, simply sprinkle on some more flour until you have a workable dough again. Knead the dough on a floured surface until it is smooth and elastic, around 8–10 minutes. This operation can be performed in a mixer, and some food processors do a fairly good job, but halve the kneading time.

Place the dough in a lightly floured bowl, slash a cross on the surface to facilitate its rising, and sprinkle on a little more flour. Loosely cover it with a plastic bag and place it in a warm, draught-free spot. Leave to rise for between 1 and 3 hours, until it has doubled in volume. Punch the dough down, sprinkling it with flour as necessary, and knead it for a minute or two. Flatten the dough and roll 30.5 cm/12 inches in diameter. Place on a baking tray.

Heat half the butter and oil in a medium-sized saucepan and cook the onions over a low heat, stirring frequently, until they start to caramelize, about 40 minutes: add the pinch of sugar towards the end. Simultaneously heat the remaining butter and oil in a frying pan, and when the foam subsides add the mushrooms, garlic and shallot. Cook for several minutes, stirring – do not worry about cooking too thoroughly,

Serves 2–3

Crust
1/2 teaspoon dried yeast or 15 g/1/2 oz
    fresh yeast
a pinch of caster sugar
200 g/7 oz strong white flour
1 level teaspoon sea salt
1 tablespoon extra virgin olive oil
approx. 125 ml/4 fl oz hand-hot water

Pizza topping
25 g/1 oz unsalted butter
2 tablespoons extra virgin olive oil
700 g/1 lb 9 oz red onions, peeled,
    halved and finely sliced
a pinch of caster sugar
225 g/8 oz girolles or other wild
    mushrooms
1 garlic clove, peeled and finely chopped
1 shallot, peeled and finely chopped
sea salt and freshly ground black pepper
125 g/4 1/2 oz blue cheese, cubed

and if they give out their juices continue cooking until these evaporate. Mix into the onions once they are cooked, and season.

Preheat the oven to 200°C fan oven/220°C or 425°F electric oven/Gas 7. Paint the pizza base with olive oil, spread the onion and mushroom mixture over to within 1 cm/½ inch of the rim, and bake for 20 minutes, sprinkling the cheese over the pizza 3 minutes before the end of cooking. Serve hot or at room temperature.

Fast

Cream of Mushroom Soup

I have refrained from calling this 'cappuccino of mushroom soup', fashionably frothy, achieved by taking an electric hand-whisk to the soup just before you serve it. But liquidizing the soup twice gives a very similar result.

Pick over the mushrooms, scrape or wipe them if they are dirty, and slice them. You will need to cook the vegetables in 2 batches: melt the butter in a large saucepan and sweat the mushrooms, onion and fennel together until soft. If the mushrooms give out their juices, reserve these along with the cooked vegetables.

Place all the cooked vegetables in the saucepan with the potato, stock, cream and seasoning, bring to the boil and simmer for 15 minutes. Liquidize the soup and reserve it in a large bowl, then liquidize it again; this time around it should emerge silky in texture and a tad frothy.

Serves 6

225 g/8 oz wild mushrooms (girolles, chanterelles, etc.)
700 g/1 lb 9 oz white mushrooms
25 g/1 oz unsalted butter
1 onion, peeled and chopped
1 small fennel bulb, trimmed and chopped
70 g/2½ oz potato, peeled and sliced
1.35 litres/2¼ pints vegetable stock
425 ml/¾ pint double cream
sea salt and freshly ground black pepper

Other Ideas

➤ Sauté a mixture of wild mushrooms, cooking them with chopped shallot and garlic, and stir in flat-leaved parsley at the end. Serve with triangles of toast, or with scrambled eggs.

➤ Sauté wild mushrooms, adding some cream at the end, and cook until they are coated in a thickened cream sauce. Serve on top of baked potatoes.

➤ Make a wild mushroom risotto, or an orzotto using pearl barley, or serve sautéd mushrooms on top of polenta with lots of melted cheese.

➤ Sauté a mixture of wild mushrooms in olive oil and leave to cool. Steep them in olive oil and a touch of red wine vinegar, and serve as an antipasto.

➤ Make a wild mushroom omelette or, even easier, a frittata.

See also:

Stuffed Cabbage with Porcini and Gruyère (page 42)
Michel Guérard's Carrot Flan – Jerusalem Artichoke Purée (page 48)
Shallot Tart Tatin (page 124)

Onions

The chopping of onions is potentially worse for a woman than for a man. The presence of mascara sees to it that not only do you weep, but you weep streams of tears speckled with black. In Laura Esquivel's *Like Water For Hot Chocolate* the book opens with the advice 'Take care to chop the onion fine. To keep from crying when you chop it (which is so annoying!), I suggest you place a little bit on your head.' This is the tip of the iceberg when it comes to folklore and how to avoid the inevitable rivers of salty tears. Dipping them first in water is one suggested remedy, placing them in the freezer is another, a problem arising should you forget to take them out. The best advice I can give is – work fast.

Given the diversity of the onion family, my use of them is comparatively simple. The bog-standard yellow onions are the ones my mother rarely commences a recipe without. I usually opt for the larger Spanish onions, even when I don't need the entire sphere; the remainder I wrap in clingfilm and store in the fridge. I choose these for their mellow flavour, and the way they collapse into a succulent, slippery mass when you sweat them in butter or olive oil.

I use red onions for salads, only the finest slivers, and also in wedges for chargrilling and barbecuing on skewers. I do sometimes cook with them too when I want an especially mild flavour – they fade to pink when you fry them.

I welcome the borettane or cipolla with open arms on the rare occasions I come across them. An element of presentation sets in here – small, about 4 cm/1½ inches across, and faintly squashed, they look wonderful as part of a casserole of young vegetables.

But it is the small pointed shallots that are to me what the yellow onion is to my mother – I so often kick off with a couple of these and a garlic clove, finely chopped and sweated, as the base of a dish. The French definitely have the edge here: they can expect to choose from silvery brown echalote grise, the deep pink echalote rose, which is far more common, and the ordinary brown ones which turn up in a variety of sizes.

Shallots are said to be like a cross between onion and garlic and not as strong as either. In my mind they are more refined than onions. I also love banana shallots, which as their name suggests are torpedo-shaped, long and pink; they can be sliced into rounds before being cooked, or roasted whole and slipped out of their skins when eaten.

I don't like a strong presence of raw onion: first, they are indigestible, and second, the aftertaste stays with you for hours. This is where spring onions come into play – just a few slivers will add spice to an appetizer of fresh goat's cheese mashed with olive oil, or to some aubergine caviar or hummus. Again I find them too overwhelming to munch on whole.

Preparation

Cutting onions into rings or crescents is fairly straightforward. What does require describing is how to dice an onion. For this peel and halve the onion vertically. Now cut in thin slices from crown to root, but not quite to the very end. Do this again at right angles, and then slice downwards so the onion collapses into dice.

Cooking

A few tips worth remembering: if you want to stop onions from colouring, cook them with salt. And when browning onions do so slowly: the flavour of caramelized brown onions is deliciously sweet and full, but they are easily burned, in which case they will be bitter. If you want to add raw onion or shallot to a dish without the full presence of the flavour, then first blanch it in boiling water.

Shallot Tart Tatin

If you can buy largish shallots it cuts down on the frustration of peeling a million tiny onions – and you could always use red onions. The tart is also nice at room temperature, but omit the mushrooms because these need to be hot.

Peel the shallots and halve or quarter, depending on size. Melt the butter in a medium-sized saucepan, add the sugar, then add the shallots and sweat over a lowish heat for 30 minutes until nicely golden and caramelized, stirring occasionally. If they begin to colour at the edges quite quickly then turn the heat down – the caramelization process should be more subtle than that.

Preheat the oven to 200°C fan oven/220°C or 425°F electric oven/ Gas 7. Add the red wine, vinegar, bay leaf and seasoning to the onions and cook until the red wine reduces right down so the onions are quite dry, amalgamating with the butter into a sauce. Remove and discard the bay leaf.

Pile the onions into a round-based 20.5 cm/8 inch mould – I use the base of a pyrex dish for this. Roll the pastry 0.25 cm/⅛ inch thick and cut to fit the surface of the onions, allowing 1 cm/½ inch for shrinkage. Press this on top of the onions and bake for 20–25 minutes until golden: once cooked, place a plate on top so that it fits closely to the pastry, and invert it. Serve warm or at room temperature.

To cook the mushrooms, heat the butter and oil in a frying pan, add the mushrooms, garlic and thyme, and fry, stirring, until soft and cooked. Now season them, pile in the centre of the tart and serve straight away.

Serves 4

Tart
500 g/1 lb 2 oz shallots
60 g/2 oz unsalted butter
1 heaped teaspoon caster sugar
200 ml/7 fl oz red wine
1 tablespoon balsamic vinegar
1 bay leaf
sea salt and freshly ground black pepper
175 g/6 oz puff pastry

Mushrooms
15 g/½ oz unsalted butter
1 tablespoon extra virgin olive oil
225 g/8 oz shiitake mushrooms, sliced if large
1 clove garlic, peeled and finely chopped
½ teaspoon thyme

Baked Red Onions with Sicilian Crumbs

Preheat the oven to 160°C fan oven/170°C or 325°F electric oven/ Gas 3, and bake the onions, unpeeled, for 1¼ hours. While they are cooking, heat the olive oil in a frying pan, add the chilli and the bread- crumbs, and cook, stirring, until they are golden and crisp; transfer to a bowl and mix in the lemon zest, capers and mint.

When the onions are cooked, slice off one end of each, squeeze the inside from its skin, arrange in a dish and slice open. Season and dot with butter, let this begin to melt, then scatter over the crumbs and serve.

Photograph between pages 104 and 105.

Serves 4

1.35 kg/3 lb red onions
3 tablespoons extra virgin olive oil
½ teaspoon red chilli, finely chopped
70 g/2½ oz white breadcrumbs
finely grated zest of 1 lemon
1 heaped dessertspoon capers, rinsed
  and coarsely chopped
6 mint leaves, finely chopped
sea salt and freshly ground black pepper
20 g/¾ oz unsalted butter

Bruschetta with Raclette and an Onion Salad

➤ Bring a large pan of salted water to the boil. Peel and halve the onions and slice finely into crescents. Add the onions to the pan, bring back to the boil and cook for 1 minute, then drain and rinse under cold running water. Place in a bowl and mix in the gherkins. Whisk the vinegar with the mustard, seasoning and sugar, and add the oil. Toss with the onions.

Preheat the grill and lightly toast the bread on both sides. Rub one side with the garlic clove. Lay the cheese on the toast and return to the grill until it is just melted. Serve with a pile of onion salad on top.

Photograph between pages 104 and 105.

Serves 4

4 × 1 cm/½ inch slices wholegrain bread
1 garlic clove, peeled
350 g/12 oz raclette cheese (weight excluding rind), sliced

Onion salad
450 g/1 lb onions
4 gherkins (40 g/1½ oz), thinly sliced
1 dessertspoon red wine vinegar
1 level teaspoon grainy mustard
sea salt and freshly ground black pepper
generous pinch of caster sugar
4 tablespoons mild olive oil

Other Ideas

➤ Include small onions in a casserole with young carrots, turnips, fennel, thin strips of chard stalks, asparagus tips, broad beans and peas, a few herb fronds, butter and a little stock.

➤ Make an onion 'marmelade' by sweating a mass of finely sliced onions in a covered pan for 35 minutes with olive oil, sugar and seasoning. Add a good shot of sherry vinegar and cook uncovered for another 30 minutes until well reduced. Serve it like a relish or a pickle. I like it best of all with blinis and sour cream.

➤ Make a salad of French beans with well-sweated onions.

➤ Braise whole peeled medium-sized onions with butter, thyme and a little stock. Remove the inside, finely chop and cook with a little cream until it thickens, then stuff the onions. These can be served at room temperature.

➤ Two of the best partners for onions are wild mushrooms and cooked and peeled chestnuts: fill little pastry cases with sliced and sweated onions, and little nibs of chestnut.

➤ Sour cream and chopped spring onion are a classic match. Serve with blinis or savoury pancakes, with spicy bean soups, and all those Mexican enchiladas and the like.

➤ There is more to pickled onions than munching them whole; just a few thin slices will act as a garnish.

➤ Crisp onion rings will serve as an accompaniment, or as part of a fritto misto: first soak them in salted milk, then dip them in flour and deep-fry them. Or just dip them into batter and deep-fry. They are also delicious in club sandwiches.

➤ Make a pissaladière with a base of puff pastry, blind-baked – spread this with onions that have been sweated down to a well-reduced mass, on top spread a homemade tomato purée, and scatter with black olives and marjoram.

See also:

Parsnips

Parsnips are not so much about variety as size. Basically they come in small, medium and large and, more curiously, long and tall: specimens that have been grown in drainpipes with a view to exhibiting them. New season offerings come through in mid-summer, when they are at their smallest, and they go on through to the following spring.

Gnarled and rather worn in appearance, parsnips make carrots look positively soigné. Indeed, carrots have a much finer texture by comparison; you certainly cannot eat parsnips uncooked. They are intensely aromatic, in fact this is their all. Many people grow up with roast parsnips around the Sunday joint, and I think this is possibly the best way of cooking them, crisp, sticky and caramelized at the edges.

Second to roasting come purées, and anything that derives thereof, such as a soufflé or a mousse. And they appreciate dairy culture: dress them up with cream, butter and cheese, and some spices. You can roast them with olive oil or chargrill cooked ones, but they don't really get a look in on the Mediterranean stakes. In fact the Italians prefer to feed them to the pigs, which could explain the special nature of Parma ham.

And therein lies an exception: I have served a salad of cooked parsnips with raisins and flat-leaved parsley, dressed with red wine vinegar and a light olive oil, with Parma ham as a starter.

Preparation

Avoid parsnips that are flaccid and bendy, and avoid soft brown patches. Peel them immediately before cooking, and remove the woody core of the older ones. You can also cook and then peel them if preferred. Because there is a difference in thickness between the tapered and the thick wedge-shaped end, I usually cut them into more or less even sticks so that they cook uniformly.

Roasted Root Vegetables with Rocket Pesto

These vegetables emerge from the oven tender and deliciously sweet. Their flavour intensifies as they roast and the peppery bitterness of the rocket is a good match. The chillies are there for the flavour they provide to the other vegetables while they're roasting, so unless you're into fire-eating don't actually eat them.

The recipe I have given is especially quick, and I often have it for supper or as a starter in the winter. For a main course I would serve some chargrilled polenta in addition.

As to the vegetables, don't use very small carrots and parsnips because they'll dry out too quickly, but nor do you want socking great specimens that will be mealy; they should be somewhere in between. A note on the pesto: it firms up if you chill it, which is fine, but bring it back to room temperature before you use it.

Preheat the oven to 180°C fan oven/190°C or 375°F electric oven/ Gas 5. Peel the carrots and parsnips and cut them up if large. Cut the skin off the celeriac and slice thickly. Remove the cores and seeds from the peppers and quarter them. Do not peel the onions. Arrange all the vegetables in a roasting dish in a single layer, pour over some olive oil, season, and roast for 50–60 minutes, stirring half-way through.

Place all the ingredients for the pesto in a food processor and reduce to a paste. Serve the roasted vegetables with a generous spoon of pesto on top.

Photograph opposite page 104.

Serves 4

350 g/12 oz carrots
350 g/12 oz parsnips
400 g/14 oz celeriac
2 red peppers
350 g/12 oz banana shallots or small
   red onions
4 red chillies
extra virgin olive oil
sea salt and freshly ground black pepper

Pesto
85 g/3 oz rocket
25 g/1 oz coriander
25 g/1 oz pine-nuts
4 tablespoons extra virgin olive oil
½ garlic clove
1 teaspoon balsamic vinegar
sea salt and freshly ground black pepper

Filo Tart with Parsnip Mousse and Mushrooms

This is more dinner party than suppertime – serve it as a starter, or as a main course with a green salad. The order of preference for the mushrooms goes girolles, ceps, chanterelles, shiitake. Obviously you could make individual tarts if you possess the right 12.5 cm/5 inch tins, or more informally you could have a croûton as the base instead of filo pastry.

To make the mousse, bring a large pan of salted water to the boil and cook the parsnips and turnips for 15 minutes. Drain into a sieve and allow surface moisture to evaporate.

Preheat the oven to 140°C fan oven/150°C or 300°F electric oven/ Gas 2. Combine the milk, cream and egg yolks in a jug; split the cardamom pod, remove the seeds and add to the jug with the seasoning. Now liquidize the cooked vegetables with the cream mixture; do this in two lots. Pass through a sieve into a large bowl, and liquidize again until it is silky smooth. Pour into a gratin dish, place in a bain-marie so that the boiling water comes three-quarters of the way up the sides, and cook for 30–40 minutes, removing it from the oven as soon as it is firm – if you leave it too long it will turn slightly curdy. Allow to cool.

Turn the oven up to 170°C fan oven/180°C or 350°F electric oven/ Gas 4. Cut the filo sheets to fit the base and sides of a 23 × 33 cm/9 × 13 inch Swiss roll tin. Paint the sheets one by one with the melted butter and layer them in the tin, cover with foil and baking beans and bake for 12–15 minutes until golden.

To serve, scoop the mousse into a bowl, whisk to a smooth, thick cream and spread this over the base of the filo. To cook the mushrooms, first clarify the butter by melting it, skim off the surface foam, reserve the clear liquid and discard the milky residue. Now heat the reserved clarified butter in a frying pan, and when it is very hot throw in the mushrooms, garlic and shallot and cook stirring constantly for several minutes. Season and stir in the parsley. Arrange on top of the parsnip mousse and serve straight away while the mushrooms are warm, though it will be good at room temperature for a couple of hours.

Serves 4–6

Mousse
450 g/1 lb parsnips, peeled
125 g/4½ oz turnip, peeled
300 ml/½ pint milk
300 ml/½ pint double cream
5 medium egg yolks
1 green cardamom pod
sea salt and freshly ground black pepper

Tart case
4 sheets of ready-made filo pastry
25 g/1 oz unsalted butter, melted

Mushrooms
40 g/1½ oz unsalted butter
225 g/8 oz mushrooms, picked over
  and sliced
1 garlic clove, peeled and finely chopped
1 shallot, peeled and finely chopped
sea salt and freshly ground black pepper
1 tablespoon coarsely chopped
  flat-leaved parsley

Seven Vegetable Tagine

This is not the sort of plateful to serve at an elegant dinner party, but it is still delicious in the wholesome fashion of minestrone or pistou. It is also a good casserole to make in quantity.

The choice and quantity of vegetables is movable, the main thing being to use the blend of spices specified in the first list of ingredients — these characterize the dish. I buy my harissa in a tube if I can, but otherwise in a tin, and keep it sealed with a layer of olive oil in the fridge. Unless the broad beans are very young and the skins are tender, you should defrost and then skin them.

Traditionally tagines are made in a shallow earthenware dish with a conical lid, called a tagine, and I have one of these in my garden with a special charcoal burner for slow-cooking such dishes. But given that a tagine is basically a casserole or a stew, it can be cooked in any suitable vessel, be it a saucepan or in a casserole in the oven. So don't be put off by not having the authentic article.

Prepare all the vegetables and have them at the ready: peel the carrots and parsnips and cut into chunky batons, peel the onions, trim the squashes, cut the cauliflower into florets.

Melt the butter in a large saucepan and add the spices, seasoning, herbs and raisins. Stir around and then add the carrots, parsnips, onions and tomato. Leave to sweat for a few minutes, add 900 ml/1½ pints of water, bring to a simmer, cover and cook for 20 minutes in total, adding the pattypans and cauliflower 6 minutes before the end. You can prepare it to this point in advance.

Add the chickpeas and broad beans and heat until the broad beans are cooked through: adjust the seasoning. Blend 150 ml/5 fl oz of the cooking liquor with the harissa and serve this separately at the table — it is very hot, so spoon it over the casserole by the teaspoon.

Serves 6

Aromatics
85 g/3 oz unsalted butter
1½ teaspoons ground ginger
1½ teaspoons ground cinnamon
½ teaspoon turmeric
25 saffron filaments
1 heaped teaspoon sea salt
½ teaspoon freshly ground black pepper
8 sprigs of coriander, tied into a bundle
8 sprigs of flat-leaved parsley, tied into a bundle
75 g/2 oz raisins

Vegetables
500g/1 lb 2 oz carrots
325 g/11 oz parsnips
325 g/11 oz baby onions
325 g/11 oz pattypan squashes, or small courgettes
1 cauliflower
700 g/1 lb 9 oz tomatoes, skinned and chopped
1 × 420 g/14 oz tin chickpeas
285 g/10 oz young frozen broad beans

For sauce
1 teaspoon harissa

Other Ideas

➤ Colcannon is usually made with mashed potato and cabbage, but in Dublin there is a version made with mashed parsnip, potato and curly kale, which gives a lovely combination of sweet parsnip and bitter cabbage.

➤ Make parsnip cakes with a purée, a little flour, seasoning and mace; dip in egg and breadcrumbs and fry.

➤ Make older parsnips into purées with cream and milk, seasoned with freshly grated nutmeg.

➤ Make mixed vegetable purées by combining parsnips with equal amounts of potato, or carrot, Jerusalem artichoke, celeriac, swede and so forth.

➤ The classic combination of game birds with parsnips can be translated into wild mushrooms with parsnips for vegetarians, given that game birds and wild mushrooms have the same musty woodland savour.

➤ Parsnip is a good pot-au-feu and tagine vegetable.

➤ Glaze cooked parsnips with butter and sugar.

➤ Parboil parsnip chips and then deep-fry them.

➤ Dress cooked parsnip with homemade mayonnaise.

Peas

When I visited San Francisco I returned almost empty-handed bar a handful of lightweight polystyrene containers crammed with a precious fodder: pea shoots. Gardeners may share my excitement over these sweet and tender pea-flavoured tips of the plant, which can be wilted in butter for an exquisite treat with scrambled eggs, or mixed into a dish of cooked peas or sautéed asparagus and morels.

The natural historian and author of the colour encyclopedia *Vegetables*, Roger Phillips, reports that in China several varieties are grown specifically for their tops, and are picked regularly to prevent them from flowering. I haven't to date seen these on sale in this country, but it only takes one enterprising grower to start the ball rolling, so perhaps in time they'll make an appearance.

For the diner peas offer fascinating diversity: there are mangetouts with their flat, tender, edible pods, and other mangetouts like the 'sugar snap' variety which are firmer and more succulent. And then there are garden peas, and 'petits pois'. Dried peas are another area, and specific varieties are grown for this purpose. The essential pea flavour is common to all these variants, so it is horses for courses, and what type you use for what dish must be judged accordingly. But it is a nice idea to combine them: mangetouts with garden peas, for example. In a similar vein, pea pods can be used to give additional flavour to a pea soup or sauce.

In cooking peas there is an element of France versus England. Traditionally we like our peas cooked with mint, while their favourite preparation involves a braised base of lettuce and onion.

Peas arrived in France from Italy in 1660 during the reign of King Henri IV – their popularity swept through the court and it was the duty of the head gardener at Versailles to produce the necessary to assuage the king's new passion. In modern times the war continues: we like ours frozen, they like theirs canned.

Sugar, salt and butter are the 'de rigueur' ingredients for peas; frankly, I can live without the mint. Spices and curry work surprisingly well: little samosas or crisp patties filled with potato and peas flavoured with some ground cloves, green cardamom and cinnamon. Bruno Loubet, chef at L'Odéon in Regent Street, cooks a dish of braised turbot fillets with a creamy sauce flavoured with curry powder, with peas and parsley in it. And curried soups like carrot or parsnip will welcome a few peas scattered over.

Cooking

As with corn, peas lose sugar in a fairly dramatic fashion within hours of being picked, converting it to starch, or simply using it up to survive. For this reason frozen peas are likely to be of a high quality, and possibly sweeter than their fresh counterparts. The message when cooking them fresh is the fresher the better.

There is one particular way of cooking peas that brings out the best in them: take 900 g/2 lb of peas in the pod, as freshly picked as possible, and shell them. In a medium-sized saucepan place 25 g/1 oz of unsalted butter, ¹/₂ teaspoon of salt, ¹/₂ teaspoon of caster sugar and 50 ml/2 fl oz of water. Bring this to a simmer over a high heat, add the peas and cook, tossing them, for 2–3 minutes. They will turn that beautiful luscious green possessed of frozen petits pois; remaining plump, they literally burst as you eat them, while being slightly buttery, sweet and salty. If you leave them even for 5 minutes after they have cooked they will wrinkle.

Petits Pois à la Française

I like to serve this with scallops added a few minutes before the end — you will need 450 g/1 lb. You could also add cooked asparagus spears, cut into 5 cm/2 inch lengths, or a poached egg, in which case omit the parsley. In the winter I have also made this with frozen peas and it's a very good and easy way of jazzing them up.

Shell the peas. Trim the base of the lettuces, remove the outer leaves and cut each into 6 wedges. Trim the leek to retain the white and pale green part and remove the tough outer layers, then cut it into fine strips 5–7.5 cm/2–3 inches long. Place the lettuce and leek in a medium-sized saucepan with the wine, stock or water, butter and seasoning. Bring to a simmer, cover, and braise for 30 minutes over a very low heat, stirring half-way through.

Place 50 ml/2 fl oz of water in a medium-sized saucepan with the butter, sugar and salt, and bring to a simmer; add the peas and cook over a high heat, tossing occasionally, for 2–3 minutes. Add them and any juices to the lettuce. Serve straight away, scattered with the parsley.

Photograph opposite page 105.

Serves 4

2 'Little Gem' lettuces
1 leek
100 ml/3½ fl oz white wine
100 ml/3½ fl oz vegetable stock or
　water
25 g/1 oz unsalted butter, diced
sea salt and freshly ground black pepper

Peas
340 g/12 oz freshly shelled peas
　(approx. 900 g/2 lb unshelled)
25 g/1 oz unsalted butter
½ teaspoon caster sugar
½ teaspoon sea salt

To serve
chopped flat-leaved parsley

Pea Soup

A virtuoso soup, straightforward to prepare and deliciously sweet and fresh. For a dinner party I recommend adding thinly sliced scallops to the soup as you take it off the heat – allow 2 per person, discarding the corals.

Shell the peas, reserving 20 of the pods; trim these of their stalks and chop. Melt the butter in a large saucepan, add the onion, and sweat until it is translucent and soft. Add the peas and chopped pods and sweat for about 1 minute. Add the wine and cook to reduce it – this should be fairly instant – then add the stock and seasoning, bring to a simmer and cook for 10 minutes.

Liquidize with the basil leaves and the cream, then pass through a sieve back into the saucepan and adjust the seasoning (it takes quite a lot of salt). Rewarm without boiling and serve with a swirl of cream and the chopped chives. The soup is also good cold.

Serves 4

900 g/2 lb fresh peas
25 g/1 oz unsalted butter
1 onion, peeled and chopped
5 tablespoons sweet white wine,
  e.g. Sauternes
750 ml/1½ pints strong vegetable stock
sea salt and freshly ground black pepper
2 basil leaves
3 tablespoons double cream

To serve
double cream
chopped chives

Poached Eggs in Sorrel Sauce with Peas

The yolk spills out into the sauce as you cut into the egg, so this one calls for lots of bread. You can use an egg poacher should you prefer it to the saucepan method.

First make the sauce: reduce the wine to a syrup (1 tablespoon) in a medium-sized saucepan, add the vegetable stock and cream, and reduce by a third. Cut the stalks out of the sorrel leaves, then wash the leaves, drain well and cut into thin strips. Season the sauce, add the sorrel and cook until it changes from bright to a dull green. Stir in the Parmesan, then the *beurre manié*, which will thicken it just a touch and give it a gloss. Add the peas to heat through.

Bring 2 large pans of water to a simmer and acidulate with a slug of vinegar. Stir the water into a lazy whirlpool and break the eggs one at a time into the water. Give them about 4 minutes in all: once they rise to the surface, trim any ragged tendrils of white. Remove with a slotted spoon, and be sure they drain thoroughly. Serve 2 eggs per person, with the sauce spooned over.

Serves 4

white wine vinegar
8 large eggs

Sauce
125 ml/4 fl oz white wine
200 ml/7 fl oz vegetable stock
200 ml/7 fl oz double cream
100 g/3½ oz sorrel
sea salt and freshly ground black pepper
2 heaped tablespoons freshly grated
   Parmesan
beurre manié, made with 1 level
   teaspoon plain flour blended with
   1 teaspoon unsalted butter
100 g/3½ oz cooked peas, fresh or
   frozen

Other Ideas

➤ Make a purée of peas flavoured with a little cream infused with saffron: serve steamed asparagus tips on top.

➤ Offset a hot, spicy dhal soup with a few sweet green peas scattered over. Make a basic lentil soup with yellow split peas or red lentils: first sweat your vegetables in olive oil or butter, then add some chopped chilli, a little ground cumin and coriander, and some vegetable stock, and cook until you have a thick soup.

➤ Flavour a potato purée with basil and serve with baby carrots, asparagus and peas.

➤ Mock up a Venetian 'risi e bisi' by making a creamy risotto and stirring in cooked peas at the end.

➤ Blanch mangetouts for 30 seconds in boiling salted water, then toss with butter and serve on top of risottos such as leek, saffron or red wine.

Peppers

The genus Capsicum covers both sweet and hot peppers, but it is the sweet types that are of concern here – large, fleshy bell peppers, as well as the tapering kinds found in Spain, and occasionally over here.

The first thing to take on board is the inbuilt colour-coding, which specifies varying degrees of ripeness, depending on the variety. Unripe they can be green – these we are familiar with – but also white, brown or purple, which are not so familiar. The green ones ripen to red, yellow and orange, again familiar, the white turn to ivory and the brown or purple ones turn a reddish-blackish purple.

I rarely use green peppers, finding them lacking in taste and indigestible, although I am fond of a particular Eastern European salad made with grilled green peppers, chopped tomato, onion, cucumber and green chilli, mixed with sour cream, which is delicious. The other occasion when I buy green peppers is when I am in Spain and can obtain the long tapering varieties, which are excellent grilled for salads.

On the whole, though, I home in on the red ones, looking for nice fat specimens that will come off well if roasted. Occasionally you come across packaged peppers advertised as 'stuffing peppers', and these I find are fleshiest of all. Always buy peppers with taut skins and very hard, crisp flesh; they shouldn't reveal any wrinkling or softness. Check the stalk too – occasionally this starts to grow fuzzy mould, in which case the pepper is none too fresh.

The skin on peppers is thick and indigestible, unless you happen to be growing your own and picking them young, so even when I am serving strips of raw pepper as crudités I peel them using a potato peeler – roasting and grilling automatically loosens the skin, as detailed below.

I can fully understand why roasted red peppers became such a hit in the eighties; deliciously sweet and slippery strips to be dressed up with olive oil, chopped parsley or basil, black olives, whole garlic cloves and salted anchovies. Ideally leave them to marinate for a day. No lemon juice or vinegar is required, instead collect the juices of the roasted peppers as you peel them and add to the salad.

Roasting

You can cook peppers under a grill or on a griddle and the skin will blister and blacken while the flesh remains nice and firm, but it's not the easiest route to skinning them, and I prefer to do them in the oven. This ensures a more even cooking, though care has to be taken not to overcook them or the flesh will go flaccid.

Place the peppers on the grid of a grill pan in a very hot oven for 20 minutes. The skin should appear loose, though not especially black. Place one plastic bag inside another and place the peppers inside. Seal the bag and leave them to cool. Once they are cool enough to handle, slip off the skin and seeds: do this working over the open plastic bag or a bowl so as to retain the juices.

It may be necessary to rinse the peppers under running water in order to remove any remaining seeds and bits of skin, and then to pat them dry, but if possible avoid this because you will lose flavour in the process. Alternatively scrape them clean using a knife. Trim the tops of the peppers, and cut into strips or leave them whole as appropriate.

Peperonata with Parmesan Shortbread

This is one of my favourite dinner party starters in the summer. I usually make the Parmesan shortbread up in double quantity – made small, they are delicious as cocktail biscuits. A poached or soft-boiled egg on top of the peperonata is another nice addition, or quail's eggs.

To make the shortbread, blend all the ingredients in a bowl or in a food processor, wrap in clingfilm and chill for 1 hour (or overnight). Heat the oven to 140°C fan oven/150°C or 300°F electric oven/Gas 2. Lightly flour a work surface, roll the dough 0.25–0.5 cm/⅛–¼ inch thick, and cut out with a 6 cm/2½ inch cutter, roll only twice. Lay on a baking sheet and cook for 30–35 minutes until a uniform light gold. Allow to cool.

While the shortbread dough is chilling, prepare the peperonata. Bring a pan of water to the boil, cut a cone from the top of each tomato to remove the core, then dip them for 20–30 seconds into the boiling water, remove to a sink of cold water and the skins should slip off with ease. Remove the seeds and coarsely chop the tomatoes. Peel the peppers using a potato peeler (don't worry about getting into the crevices), remove the core and seeds and cut into thin strips.

Heat the olive oil in a large saucepan and sweat the onion and garlic until translucent and soft. Add the peppers, cover and allow to sweat in their own juices for 10 minutes. Add the tomatoes, seasoning and vinegar and simmer uncovered over a low heat until the peppers are coated in a thick, reduced sauce. This will take 1½–2 hours – don't rush it, just give it a stir every now and again taking special care that it doesn't burn at the end. Adjust the salt, and serve warm or at room temperature with the Parmesan shortbread.

Photograph opposite page 152.

Serves 4

***

Parmesan shortbread
100 g/3½ oz unsalted butter
50 g/1¾ oz freshly grated Parmesan
100 g/3½ oz plain flour
50 g/1¾ oz ground almonds
⅛ teaspoon cayenne pepper
sea salt

Peperonata
900 g/2 lb beefsteak tomatoes
8 (approx. 1.5 kg/3 lb 5 oz) red and
    yellow peppers
3 tablespoons extra virgin olive oil
1 large onion, peeled and chopped
2 garlic cloves, peeled and chopped
sea salt and freshly ground black pepper
2 teaspoons balsamic vinegar

Roasted Red Pepper Soup

Preheat the oven to 200°C fan oven/220°F or 425°F electric oven/ Gas 7. Remove the core and seeds from the peppers and quarter them. Place in a roasting tray, drizzle over half the olive oil and roast for 25–30 minutes until soft and beginning to colour.

In the meantime, sweat the onion, chilli, carrots and celery in the remaining olive oil over a low heat in a large saucepan for 10 minutes. Add the tomatoes, peppers, stock and seasoning and simmer for 20 minutes. Add the saffron water, liquidize the soup in a blender and pass through a sieve. Adjust the seasoning, and serve with a spoonful of sour cream and some chopped coriander in the centre.

Serves 4

900 g/2 lb red peppers
4 tablespoons extra virgin olive oil
1 onion, peeled and chopped
$\frac{1}{3}$ teaspoon finely chopped red chilli
175 g/6 oz carrots, peeled and sliced
1 heart of celery, sliced
450 g/1 lb tomatoes, chopped
1.2 litres/2 pints vegetable stock
sea salt and freshly ground black pepper
15 saffron filaments, ground in a pestle
   and mortar and infused with
   1 tablespoon boiling water

To serve
150 ml/5 fl oz sour cream
2 tablespoons chopped coriander

Red Peppers Roasted with Cherry Tomatoes

This is not new at all. I included it in my first book, *A Feast of Flavours*, and I am including it again here because so many friends have told me how often they cook it. As the peppers cook, the juice from the tomatoes combines with the juice from the peppers, merging with the honey and olive oil into a delicious liquor which calls for some good bread.

The peppers are nicest served warm, and you can make an attractive arrangement by using half orange and half red peppers, and filling them with different coloured tomatoes: choose from red, yellow or orange.

Cut the peppers in half from the stem to the base, leaving the green stalk. Remove the seeds and pith. Halve the cherry tomatoes and fill the pepper cavities with these. Place on a baking tray, dribble over the honey and a little olive oil, season with salt and pepper, and bake them in a very hot oven for 20–30 minutes, until the peppers are wilted and patched with brown. Serve garnished with the parsley.

Serves 3–6

3 red peppers
350 g/12 oz cherry tomatoes
3 teaspoons runny honey
olive oil
sea salt and freshly ground black pepper

To serve
flat-leaved parsley

Other Ideas

➤ For a salad that promises a wonderful texture, peel, halve and slice some onions and fry them in olive oil with some chopped garlic for about 8 minutes until soft and beginning to colour. Mix with strips of roasted pepper and leave to marinate with some basil leaves. Serve at room temperature, with goat's cheese and black olives.

➤ Roast red peppers, skin and deseed them. Stuff them with a well-flavoured mixture of pine-nuts, parsley, mint, brioche crumbs, lemon zest and haloumi cheese, and return to the oven for 10–15 minutes. Serve after they have cooled a little, with more olive oil poured over.

➤ Make a romesco sauce with roasted red peppers: first make a paste with fried bread, garlic, chilli, roasted peppers, roasted and ground almonds and tomatoes, then add olive oil until you have a sauce the consistency of mayonnaise, and sharpen with red wine vinegar. This is delicious with grilled and barbecued chicken and fish, and grilled vegetables.

➤ Simple crostini can be made with a base of French bread fried in olive oil, topped with strips of red pepper and goat's cheese, and some basil.

➤ Roasted peppers have an affiliation with pesto, particularly on top of a pizza.

➤ Use red, orange and yellow peppers together in salads for a wonderful blaze of contrasting colours.

See also:

Aubergine and Mozzarella Rolls – Pesto Dressing (page 17)
Red Pepper and Celeriac Charlotte (page 60)
Spaghetti with Red Pepper Pesto (page 73)
Roasted Root Vegetables with Rocket Pesto (page 130)
Sauté of Butternut Squash, Red Pepper and Rocket with Eggs (page 170)

Potatoes

There is a wonderful entry on potatoes in the Wine and Food Society's *Concise Encyclopaedia of Gastronomy*, published in 1941, that runs: 'Potatoes are with us all the year round, new, not so new, or old. They are full of everything that is good for good people. But, unlike good people, whose goodness is in the heart, most of the goodness in the potato is in the skin. Potatoes are not only full of goodness, but again, unlike many people who are ever so good, potatoes are not boring.'

Quite. The days of reds and whites are all but over, partly because it is now the law to specify what variety of potato is on sale. *The Story of the Potato* by Alan Wilson leaves no doubt as to the depth of this subject, although it is a telling fact that two-thirds of earlies grown commercially, and half of the maincrops, are represented by six varieties between them, when there are literally hundreds of varieties, each differing in shape, colour, texture and flavour.

I count myself among the ranks of that select band of enthusiasts, the potato eaters, although my experience goes no further than what any large supermarket has on offer, backed up by more specialized greengrocers. That is, I do not have a vegetable garden, and have not tasted many of the rarer varieties available to those with green fingers.

If you are a gardener, seed companies can provide some exciting options, and by far the greatest potato star was the late Donald MacLean of Dornock Farm, Crieff, Perthshire, who had a collection of over 400 varieties. This is no mean feat when you consider that unlike other seeds, seed potatoes cannot be stored in a refrigerator but have to be grown from scratch every year.

Even at supermarket level, though, there is considerable choice over the period of a year. To start with, potatoes divide into 'first earlies', 'second earlies' and 'maincrop'. Just to confuse the issue, 'new' potatoes as you well know can now be found for sale even in January – varieties like 'Ratte', 'Charlotte' and 'Belle de Fontenay'. Alan Wilson comments: 'Our nineteenth-century forefathers appreciated this type of potato. Most large estates relied on their expert gardeners to produce potatoes of a waxy texture in mid-season, the aim being to provide potatoes which tasted like new ones. These are known today under the general term of "salad potatoes". Alternatively real new potatoes could be produced at Christmas from greenhouse or cloche plantings, using seed taken from the early crop.'

The differences between potatoes are not so apparent in terms of flavour as in texture. The red-skinned 'Romano' is quite floury and carries with it a flavour of baked potatoes even when boiled. 'King Edward' is mealy, a lovely velvety boiled potato. 'Maris Piper' produces a very white, fluffy purée with a better flavour than 'King Edward'. 'Charlotte' turns into a rich, dense and earthy purée, even though traditionalists would argue that waxy potatoes should not be used for this purpose. Observations are endless. But apart from dividing potatoes into earlies or salad potatoes, and maincrop, the point is to enjoy their differences.

Peeling

This is not something which needs instruction, just a brief word on peelers. I do not know whether it is because I am left-handed, but I find the French swivel style of peeler that looks like a bar across a horseshoe to be by far the most efficient. Beware any other peelers that remove too much potato with the peel.

Truffled Artichokes and New Potatoes

I had this as a starter at Le Caprice restaurant in Piccadilly: a sauté of new potatoes and Jerusalem artichokes, flavoured with truffle oil, with a few stray leaves of wilted spinach. Truffle oil is quite 'restaurant' — don't be deterred if you can't get it. And, should you happen to come across them you could include a handful of the miniature spiralled Japanese artichokes, or crosnes.

Bring 2 large pans of salted water to the boil, and acidulate a bowl of water for the artichokes as you peel them. Peel the artichokes and the potatoes and boil simultaneously until just tender; the precise cooking time of each will depend on their size. Drain them into a colander and run some cold water over them so they are cool enough to handle. Slice thickly, about 1 cm/½ inch. Chop and crush the garlic clove to a paste with a sprinkling of salt.

Heat the 2 oils in 2 frying pans or a wok, add the garlic, and moments later add the potatoes and artichokes. Season, and cook for 10–15 minutes until golden in patches, turning them quite constantly but with care so as not to break up the artichoke slices. Toss in the spinach at the end of cooking — the heat of the vegetables will wilt the leaves. Serve straight away.

Serves 4

lemon juice or white wine vinegar
700 g/1 lb 9 oz Jerusalem artichokes
700 g/1 lb 9 oz new potatoes
1 garlic clove, peeled
sea salt
2 tablespoons extra virgin olive oil
1 tablespoon truffle oil
freshly ground black pepper
100 g/3½ oz young spinach leaves

Baked Potatoes with Oil and Parsley

This derives from Alain Ducasse's lumpy mashed potato as served at Monte's club in Sloane Street. It oozes olive oil and is speckled green with masses of parsley and a little garlic – here it is inside a baked potato.

If you are honouring bonfire night, serve these with baked beans and an additional knob of butter stirred into them. When travelling through France I kept an emergency supply of baked beans to hand in case the menu wasn't child-friendly: a look of respect would come over the waiter's face when I produced the can. He would nod his recognition – 'Aah, les baked beans' – and the service would be good thereafter.

Preheat the oven to 200°C fan oven/220°C or 425°F electric oven/ Gas 7. Scrub the potatoes and dry them. Make an incision the shape of a lid on the top of each one with a small sharp knife. Place a little olive oil in the palm of your hand, rub your hands together, and then rub over the potatoes, coating each one lightly with the oil. Place them on a baking dish and sprinkle over some crystals of sea salt. Bake for 1¼ hours.

Remove the potato lid from each potato, scoop out the inside into a bowl and loosely mash with the other filling ingredients. Refill the potatoes and replace the lid. You can rewarm the potatoes, but gently so as not to ruin the flavour of the oil.

Serves 4

Potatoes
4 × 225 g/8 oz maincrop potatoes
extra virgin olive oil
sea salt

Filling
5 tablespoons extra virgin olive oil
2 heaped tablespoons chopped
    flat-leaved parsley
½ garlic clove, peeled and crushed to a
    paste with salt
sea salt and freshly ground black pepper

Potato and Emmental Gratin

This is a really rich, gooey pie with a crusty golden surface. Emmental is one of the classic cooking cheeses – it melts in a particular fashion and has a very distinctive flavour. A green salad is all that is required to accompany it, with either an olive oil or a walnut oil dressing.

Preheat the oven to 180°C fan oven/190°C or 375°F electric oven/ Gas 5. Combine all the liquids in a jug and season with salt, pepper and nutmeg. Peel the potatoes and slice finely; you can do this with a food processor attachment. Butter a 35.5 × 25.5 × 5 cm/14 × 10 × 2 inch oven-proof dish.

You need three layers each of potato and cheese, layering as follows: first lay the potatoes in rows so the slices overlap. Season, sprinkle with cheese, and scatter over a few garlic cloves and a bay leaf. Drizzle over a quarter of the liquid. Continue with the remaining ingredients, ending with cheese; compress the layers with your hands before pouring over the remaining liquor. The garlic, however, should be used up within the first two layers so there is none on the surface – this is to avoid it burning.

Cook the gratin for 1 hour, until the potatoes are tender and the top is golden and bubbling. Serve in wedges.

Photograph between pages 152 and 153.

Serves 6

425 ml/¾ pint double cream
150 ml/5 fl oz milk
50 ml/2 fl oz vegetable stock
100 ml/3½ fl oz white wine
sea salt, freshly ground black pepper
   and nutmeg
1.6 kg/3½ lb maincrop potatoes,
   i.e. Maris Piper
450 g/1 lb grated Emmental
10 whole garlic cloves, peeled
3 bay leaves

New Potatoes with Taleggio and Crème Fraîche

I like making this with the very first tiny Jersey Royals. It's a really quick supper dish, and fairly indulgent; taleggio succumbs to heat in the way of all the best melting cheeses, such as raclette, and collapses into a creamy mass.

Bring a pan of salted water to the boil. Cut the potatoes to the same size and cook until tender. Drain them and put to one side.

Heat the crème fraîche, mascarpone and mustard gently in a small saucepan. Add the taleggio and after about a minute toss with the potatoes. Serve scattered with chives.

It's important that the cheese doesn't completely melt into the cream but just warms through and holds its shape, so it's a case of throwing it all together quickly.

Serves 4

700 g/1 lb 9 oz new potatoes, scrubbed
   or peeled
50 g/2 oz crème fraîche
50 g/2 oz mascarpone
½ teaspoon Dijon mustard
150 g/5 oz taleggio, sliced thinly
snipped chives

Other Ideas

➤ When making a potato salad, dress it while hot with white wine and extra virgin olive oil, then once it is cool add chopped herbs and spring onions and leave overnight for the flavours to develop.

➤ The best roast potatoes are those with a really thick, crispy exterior and melting interior. To achieve this, first parboil them for about 10 minutes until they are half-way to being cooked. Then drain and shake them in the pan until they appear quite floury. Place in a roasting tray, pour over some extra virgin olive oil, scatter over coarse grain sea salt and roast in a hot oven for about 1 hour.

➤ New potatoes are also delicious roasted. Parboil them in their skins for about 8 minutes, then drain and place in a roasting tray, pour over some extra virgin olive oil and sprinkle with sea salt and thyme; roast for 1 hour in a moderate oven.

➤ For sauté potatoes, slice cooked potatoes and fry them for about 20 minutes in olive oil, adding some chopped garlic towards the end, and some coarsely chopped flat-leaved parsley at the very end. There should be masses of crispy bits.

➤ Potato purées can be made with either new or maincrop potatoes. The texture obtained from each is very different – with new potatoes it tends to be firm and fine, and with maincrop potatoes lighter and more grainy. I usually enrich it either with crème fraîche alone, or with a mixture of extra virgin olive oil and double cream, and occasionally a little butter for good measure. Or, more classically, with hot milk and butter. There is no doubt that the finest potato purées are not very good for you.

See also:

Caldo Verde (page 45)
Spiced Celeriac Mash (page 61)
Potatoes with Onion in Olive Oil (page 72)
Fennel Brandade with Samphire (page 158)

Rocket

Rocket (arugula to the Americans) was one of the defining leaves of the eighties. Having discovered it via the Mediterranean, we could not get enough of its slightly bitter and peppery wavy-edged leaves. I cannot count the number of starters I have eaten in recent years that have arrived 'on a bed of rocket'.

Rocket is a cress, also known as Italian cress, and Italy is indeed a big user. It is more pungent than watercress – I have been served salads of pure rocket dressed with olive oil and lemon juice that I have found overwhelming. I prefer it tempered with a mix of other leaves, such as in that masterful Provençal blend 'mesclun', a mix of mild and bitter leaves that includes dandelion, and sometimes chervil.

Generally the larger the leaf the stronger-flavoured it tends to be. I look for small and tender leaves. It is daft that it should be sold in those small herb pouches in supermarkets when we use it as a salad leaf, because it makes it so expensive to use any quantity. Whenever possible try to find it sold loose (my greengrocer does this). I have also come across 'wild' rocket – its leaves are longer and the lobes much smaller, and it is even more peppery than the cultivated type.

Try to buy and use rocket while it is very fresh; it quickly yellows at the edges. Trim it of tough stalks and give it a good wash to dislodge any sand. Basically it is a cool weather crop, so the spring and autumn are good times for eating it.

Peperonata with Parmesan Shortbread (page 140)

Saffron Risotto with Samphire (page 160)

Potato and Emmental Gratin (page 148)

Turnip and Rocket Risotto

Being yellow in colour, this could pass as a saffron risotto; in fact it is the turmeric that lends its colour.

Peel and grate the turnips, and peel and finely chop the onion. Bring the vegetable stock to the boil and keep it simmering while cooking the risotto.

Melt the butter in a large heavy-bottomed pan and sweat the onion over a low heat until it is soft and translucent – it should not colour. Add the grated turnip and sweat this until it is wilted and beginning to soften. Now add the rice and the turmeric and cook for about 1 minute until it is translucent. Add the wine and allow the rice to absorb it. Start to add the simmering stock in ladles; at no stage should the rice be flooded.

Finish the risotto while the rice is still firm: stir in the Parmesan and the cream – the consistency should be loose. Season the risotto with salt, pepper and lemon juice and toss in the rocket; the heat of the risotto will wilt the leaves. Serve immediately.

Serves 4

350 g/12 oz turnips
1 small onion
1.2 litres/2 pints vegetable stock
60 g/2 oz unsalted butter
325 g/11 oz risotto rice, e.g. Arborio or
    Carnaroli
$\frac{1}{2}$ teaspoon turmeric
150 ml/5 fl oz white wine
60 g/2 oz freshly grated Parmesan
125 ml/4 fl oz double cream, whipped
sea salt and freshly ground black pepper
squeeze of lemon juice
2 large handfuls of rocket leaves

Rocket and Potato Soup with Blue Cheese Croûtons

This is a lovely green, peppery soup, and a doddle to make. The only precondition is that you should be able to obtain rocket in a large bunch rather than in those silly herb pouches that cost the earth. You can use Stilton, Gorgonzola, Roquefort, Fourme d'Ambert or any other creamy blue cheese.

Melt the butter in a saucepan and cook the rocket briefly until it wilts. Add the potato and cook 1 minute longer. Add the boiling water, bring to the boil immediately, season, and cook for 6 minutes. Liquidize, pass through a sieve and adjust the seasoning.

Heat the grill. Lay the cheese on the croûtons and grill until beginning to melt – float these in the soup.

Serves 4

40 g/1½ oz unsalted butter
300 g/10½ oz coarsely chopped rocket
225 g/8 oz potato, peeled and finely
  sliced
1.2 litres/2 pints boiling water or
  vegetable stock
sea salt and freshly ground black pepper

To serve
100–125 g/3½–4½ oz blue cheese,
  sliced
8 thin slices French bread from a thin
  loaf, toasted

Egg Mayonnaise Sandwiches

Bring a pan of water to the boil and cook the eggs for 8 minutes, then run cold water into the pan until they are cool. Shell them, cutting off and discarding the top of the white (unless you happen to be especially partial to white – I prefer yolk). Chop the remaining egg quite finely.

In a bowl whisk the mustard with the egg yolk, then start to whisk in the oil, very gradually to begin with until the mayonnaise 'takes'. It should be extremely thick by the end. Add a squeeze of lemon juice and season. Stir in the chopped egg.

Assemble the sandwiches with the egg mayonnaise, spring onion and rocket, and cut each round into 4 triangles.

Makes 6 rounds

8 eggs
¾ teaspoon Dijon mustard
1 medium egg yolk
150–225 ml/5–8 fl oz groundnut oil
squeeze of lemon juice
sea salt and freshly ground black pepper
12 slices buttered granary bread
4 spring onions, trimmed and thinly
    sliced
2 handfuls of rocket, sliced in half

Other Ideas

➤ Serve it as the base for toasted goat's cheese – a classic marriage.

➤ Being a strong leaf, it needs to be dressed with a slightly tart vinaigrette: balsamic vinegar and olive oil 1:7, or a walnut vinaigrette.

➤ Rocket loves the addition of other characterful ingredients like black olives, Roquefort, anchovies and caperberries (alcaparras – the pickled berry of the caper bush that looks like a rugby ball on a stalk). As a foil for its heat, mix in some slices of avocado.

➤ Chop rocket leaves and toss them at the last minute into potatoes sautéed with garlic. Or any other vegetable stir-fry.

➤ Wilt rocket with garlic and chilli, and stir in some cooked pasta – serve with grated Parmesan.

➤ If you want to make a herb filling for ravioli, include rocket as one of the leaves.

➤ Make rocket sandwiches with white bread and unsalted butter.

See also:

Salad of Jerusalem Artichokes, Rocket and Hazelnuts (page 104)
Roasted Root Vegetables with Rocket Pesto (page 130)
Sauté of Butternut Squash, Red Pepper and Rocket with Eggs (page 170)

Samphire

Marsh samphire looks as though it should be growing underwater in *The Little Mermaid*, with its plump, almost comical green fronds that grow upwards cactus-fashion. It is found growing wild on salt marshes, from whence it derives its distinctive brackish savour. Once upon a time it was used in the manufacture of glass, which accounts for its other common name, glasswort.

However, it is not to be confused with rock samphire as referred to in *King Lear*: 'half-way down hangs one that gathers samphire, dreadful trade'. The very thought induces vertigo. This hangs tassel-like from cliffs and rocks, and it too is edible, though I have never tried it – spring is the right time, before it flowers. Once upon a time it was cultivated in English gardens; sometimes known as 'crest marine', it was popular as a pickle. This is the true samphire.

Traditionally marsh samphire was ready for picking on the longest day of the year in June, and is past its best by September. Such is the modern demand for this vegetable that, weather providing, you can usually find it from the end of April through to October. Though I would advise stopping in August, since a fibrous core develops in the fronds which makes for stringy eating.

Fishmongers are a good hunting ground for samphire, and so are specialized or upmarket greengrocers, though if you live close to a shoreline where it grows it is easy enough to recognize. On a visit to Billingsgate I came across samphire that had been cultivated in India. It was pretty vile – I suspect any attempts to farm it in the future may not produce such great results.

While you can eat the young and tender fronds raw, I prefer to blanch them for 30 seconds in boiling water. Recipes often suggest boiling samphire, but this is misleading – it is not a vegetable that requires cooking as such, and its quality lies with its unique, crunchy texture.

It should be said that a little goes a long way. It is concentrated in flavour, and the salinity is marked. I rarely serve it alone, though a small pile blanched and dressed with melted butter and eaten with some brown bread makes a great treat. It is a wonderful vegetable for serving with fish and, because of its association with the sea, it is particularly valuable for the vegetarian.

Selection

Stalks of samphire should snap easily between your thumbnail and finger, otherwise they will be too tough to eat. I have bought samphire in varying conditions, but the main thing is to avoid it if it appears slimy, which means it is past its best and will be hell to pick over.

Preparation

Pick it over carefully, removing tough, damaged or slimy stems. Wash it twice in a sink of cold water. It will float to the top while the grunge sinks, so this is quite easy. If you prepare it on the day you buy it, it will keep for several days in a covered bowl in the fridge.

Fennel Brandade with Samphire

This is a quite a strong, rich purée – I usually serve croûtons in addition.

Trim the fennel of any discoloured bits and quarter vertically. Place the fennel, garlic and thyme in a large saucepan with the wine, water and seasoning; bring to the boil, cover and simmer for 30 minutes. Effectively you will be steaming the fennel. Check towards the end to make sure it hasn't boiled dry, and add a little more water if necessary.

Simultaneously bring a pan of salted water to the boil, peel the potatoes, boil them until tender, then drain them.

Discard the thyme and place the fennel, garlic, olive oil and cream in a liquidizer and reduce to a purée. You will need to do this in two lots. Pass the purée through a sieve. Press the potatoes through a sieve too, and blend with the fennel purée: adjust the seasoning. You can prepare this in advance.

To serve, reheat the fennel brandade over a low heat. Do not boil it vigorously or you will ruin the oil. Bring a large pan of water to the boil, blanch the samphire for 30 seconds, then strain it, return it to the pan and add the butter so that it melts. Smooth the brandade over the base of 4 warm plates and scatter the samphire on top.

Serves 4

4 large fennel bulbs
5 garlic cloves, peeled
5 sprigs of thyme
300 ml/½ pint white wine
100 ml/3½ fl oz water
sea salt and freshly ground black pepper
225 g/8 oz new potatoes
225 ml/8 fl oz extra virgin olive oil
50 ml/2 fl oz double cream
400 g/14 oz samphire, picked over
15 g/½ oz unsalted butter

Samphire Blinis

Unlike the really thick blinis, these are fairly delicate, lacy affairs, set with green streaks of samphire. Serve them as a first course with crème fraîche or sour cream, or, even better, with some smoked salmon, at which point they become quite substantial.

Blend the yeast with half the milk, then whisk to a smooth paste with half the flour, the salt and the sugar; cover with a plate and leave in a warm place (75°F) for 1 hour until doubled in volume. Whisk in the remaining milk, flour, butter, oil and egg yolks and leave to prove for another hour. Whisk the egg whites until stiff and fold into the batter. Leave to stand for 20 minutes.

While you wait for the blinis, pick over the samphire, removing any tough, damaged or slimy stems, and wash twice in a sink of cold water. Bring a large pan of water to the boil and blanch the samphire for 30 seconds, then drain into a sieve and run cold water through it; reserve.

To cook the blinis, select a heavy-duty cast-iron, or well-seasoned frying pan; I usually have two on the go at once. Give it an initial brush with groundnut oil – there is no need to oil it thereafter because of the butter in the batter. Heat the pan over a medium heat, whisk the batter thoroughly, and ladle it into the pan so that it spreads to a diameter of 12.5–15 cm/5–6 inches. Scatter over some of the samphire. After about 45 seconds, when it appears pitted and almost dry on the topside, turn it using a palette knife and cook for another 45 seconds. Practise with the first blini and if necessary discard it. Stack the blinis on a plate and cover with foil to keep them warm. You can rewarm them in a low oven.

Serves 4
(makes 12 × 15 cm/6 inch blinis)

---

7 g/¼ oz fresh yeast or equivalent dried
425 ml/¾ pint lukewarm milk
175 g/6 oz strong white flour
½ teaspoon salt
1 level teaspoon caster sugar
60 g/2 oz unsalted butter, melted
1 tablespoon groundnut oil
2 medium eggs, separated
300 g/10½ oz samphire

Saffron Risotto with Samphire

Pick over the samphire, removing any tough or slimy stalks, and wash thoroughly in two changes of cold water.

Heat the stock in a small saucepan and keep it just below a simmer while cooking the risotto. Heat 50 g/1¾ oz of the butter in a heavy-bottomed pan and sweat the onion over a low heat until it is translucent and soft; it must not colour. Add the rice and cook for 1–2 minutes. Pour in the wine and continue to cook until it has been absorbed. Add the saffron liquid and start to pour in ladles of simmering stock – at no stage should the rice be flooded. It will take about 25 minutes to cook. Stop cooking the risotto while it is still too moist, because it will continue to absorb moisture while you finish it off and serve it.

Half-way through cooking the risotto, bring a large pan of water to the boil. When the risotto finishes cooking, blanch the samphire for 30 seconds, then drain it.

Stir the Parmesan and the remaining butter into the risotto and adjust the seasoning. Lastly, stir in the whipped cream – it is this that will give it a really rich texture. Serve with a pile of samphire in the centre.

Photograph between pages 152 and 153.

Serves 4

225 g/8 oz samphire
1 litre/1¾ pints vegetable stock
70 g/2½ oz unsalted butter
1 onion, peeled and finely chopped
325 g/11 oz risotto rice
150 ml/5 fl oz white wine
25 saffron filaments, ground and blended
    with 1 tablespoon of boiling water
60 g/2 oz freshly grated Parmesan
sea salt and freshly ground white pepper
150 ml/5 fl oz double cream, whipped

Other Ideas

➤ Make samphire into fritters to serve with ratatouille or aubergine caviar.

➤ Blanch samphire and serve it with hollandaise. Or drizzle a sabayon over it – this is similar to hollandaise, made by whisking egg yolks and wine over simmering water until frothy, then adding melted butter to give you a much lighter sauce: for 175 g/6 oz of unsalted butter, use 2 egg yolks and 50 ml/2 fl oz of white wine.

➤ Sauté some mushrooms with garlic and throw samphire into the pan at the end.

➤ Blanch and refresh samphire in cold water and serve it around some crab and potato dressed with mayonnaise.

➤ Serve samphire hot over boiled haricot or butter beans, smothered in a lemon butter sauce.

➤ Stir it into a Thai hot and sour fish soup.

➤ Fry it in a wok with garlic, ginger, chilli and sesame oil.

Spinach

While at university, perhaps a reaction to all that hard living, I craved spinach. Really craved it; I would ask friends travelling up from London to York if they could bring me a delivery. York, in those days, it seemed, had not seen it tinned, let alone fresh. It remains one of my favourite vegetables. I can sit down to a bowl of freshly cooked leaves, with a large knob of butter and some seasoning, and eat just that.

It is quite usual to be able to buy both mature spinach and the young leaves, which fetch a premium. I first encountered these tender young leaves (or 'pousse d'épinard') in my days as a chef, and was instantly hooked. These, primarily, are intended for salads, particularly warm ones where the leaves are robust enough to withstand a hot oil, but equally I enjoy them cooked.

I would be fibbing if I said I never use frozen spinach. But its texture is nothing compared to the fresh. It is much tougher, and I would not allow it the minimal treatment of a drop of cream and a little garlic. It does, however, pass if you are combining it with cheese, mushrooms and so forth and stuffing a baked potato, for instance.

I particularly like spinach dressed up with butter, cream, garlic or nutmeg, and cheese and eggs. But it also behaves well in Pacific Rim cookery, so consider Eastern touches: sesame oil, soy sauce and chilli.

Gardeners should consider growing New Zealand spinach, which is not a true spinach but is similar in flavour, with plump, heart-shaped leaves which hold their texture when cooked.

Selection

It is easy to tell if spinach is fresh. The leaves will be squeaky and pert; if they look like tired old rags then they are past their best. Also beware of the prepacks – these often remain on the shelves too long, and some of the leaves may be slimy. Once this happens the whole bag becomes tainted. If you are buying and keeping a prepack overnight, store it in the bottom of the fridge and open the bag to let it breathe.

Preparation

Mature spinach is usually sold loose, so you can avoid the prepack problem. It requires a more thorough cleaning than the young leaves; give it 2 rough and tumble washes in a large sink of cold water. Strip the leaves off any tough stalks and discard these, and if the leaves are very large then tear or slice them into wide strips.

Cooking

Spinach shrinks beyond belief when cooked: 450 g/1 lb per person is not overdoing it. Allow about 110 g/4 oz per person for a salad. **Method 1:** Bring a large pan of salted water to the boil and fill a sink with cold water. Plunge the washed spinach into the boiling water, bring to a simmer and cook for 1 minute. Drain and cool in the sink. Using your hands, wring out the spinach into balls. These can be reheated with a knob of butter and some seasoning when required. **Method 2:** Wash the spinach and place it in a saucepan over a low heat with just the water that clings to the leaves. Cover and steam it for 5 minutes, stirring half-way through. Drain into a sieve, pressing out the excess water. Serve with a knob of butter and seasoning, or a dash of cream and a little garlic crushed to a paste with salt. **Method 3:** Wash the spinach and drain it thoroughly. Heat a knob of butter or some olive oil in a frying pan, add a mound of leaves and cook, tossing them constantly with 2 spoons until they have wilted. Remove to a dish or bowl and season them. If there are any juices left in the frying pan, drain these, and repeat the process with the remaining spinach.

Spinach and Feta Appetizer

This is a mezze style salad-cum-dip to load on to toasted pitta bread, or tortillas, with some olives on the side. It is worth grinding your own cumin seeds in a coffee grinder – they'll keep for several weeks.

Heat the olive oil in a large saucepan, add the onion and the salt, and cook over a low heat for 8 minutes until the onion is soft and cooked – do not let it colour. Add the spices, and moments later add half the spinach and turn the heat to medium. Stir, cover, and cook for about 1 minute until the spinach has wilted. Add the remaining spinach, and cook likewise until it wilts. Season with pepper and allow to cool to room temperature. Drain off any excess liquid and place the spinach in a bowl. Stir in the olive oil and the lemon juice. Mix in the feta or serve it separately.

Photograph opposite page 153.

Serves 4

3 tablespoons extra virgin olive oil
1 large red onion, peeled, halved and
    sliced
½ teaspoon sea salt
½ teaspoon ground cumin seeds
½ teaspoon ground coriander seeds
350 g/12 oz young spinach leaves
freshly ground black pepper

To serve
3 tablespoons extra virgin olive oil
squeeze of lemon juice
110 g/4 oz feta cheese, crumbled

Warm Quail's Eggs and Spinach

Quail's eggs, barely set on the inside, sit in a creamy broth flavoured with saffron, with young, wilted spinach leaves. This makes a rich yet light first or main course. Allow plenty of bread for mopping up.

Bring a small pan of water to the boil and cook the quail's eggs for 2½ minutes, then run cold water into the pan until they are cold. Remove and carefully shell them, with the assistance of a small paring knife to pierce the membrane if it proves obstinate. Reserve the shelled eggs in a bowl of cold water until required.

Melt the butter in a medium-sized saucepan and sweat the spinach leaves until they wilt. Add the white wine and reduce right down. Add the vegetable stock and cream, bring to the boil, and simmer for a couple of minutes. Stir in the saffron and seasoning. You can prepare the sauce to this point in advance.

To serve, reheat the sauce, stir in the *beurre manié* (it should thicken instantly but only slightly), add the quail's eggs and heat them through for a minute. Serve in warm shallow bowls.

Serves 4

24 quail's eggs
15 g/½ oz unsalted butter
350 g/12 oz young spinach leaves
150 ml/5 fl oz white wine
225 ml/8 fl oz double-strength vegetable stock
200 ml/7 fl oz double cream
20 saffron filaments, ground and blended with 1 tablespoon boiling water
sea salt and freshly ground black pepper
1 teaspoon *beurre manié*, made by mashing together equal amounts of unsalted butter and plain flour

Spinach Roulade with Herbed Mascarpone

This is a good dinner party starter. I usually serve it with smoked salmon, but thin slices alone will do fine for vegetarians, with a few sprigs of watercress to garnish.

Heat the oven to 180°C fan oven/190°C or 375°F electric oven/Gas 5. Wash the spinach (even if the packet says don't) and place the leaves, with the parsley, in a large saucepan. Cover and cook over a medium heat for a few minutes until the spinach wilts. Place in a sieve and press out all the excess water. Cool to room temperature.

Reduce the spinach to a purée in a food processor with the egg yolks, flour, Parmesan, garlic and seasoning. Remove to a large bowl. Whisk the egg whites in a separate bowl, and gradually fold into the spinach mixture.

Line a baking sheet with paper parchment and butter it. Using a palette knife, spread the mixture in a square about 30.5 × 30.5 cm/12 × 12 inches. Bake for 10 minutes until set. Remove and allow to cool, then trim to a square 28 × 28 cm/11 × 11 inches.

Blend all the ingredients for the mascarpone in a bowl. Spread the spinach layer with the mascarpone and roll up. Chill until required, and serve in slices 1 cm/½ inch thick.

Serves 6

Spinach layer
450 g/1 lb spinach
25 g/1 oz parsley leaves
4 medium eggs, separated
1 tablespoon plain flour
40 g/1½ oz freshly grated Parmesan
½ garlic clove
sea salt and freshly ground black pepper

Mascarpone filling
450 g/1 lb mascarpone
3 heaped tablespoons finely chopped
    herbs: chives, marjoram, basil,
    parsley, coriander, tarragon
1 tablespoon finely chopped white of
    spring onion
squeeze of lemon juice
sea salt
few drops of Tabasco

Other Ideas

➤ Wilt the spinach in olive oil and serve with cooked chickpeas or butter beans, with more olive oil poured over, some chopped shallots and seasoning.

➤ Dress raw young leaves with olive oil and season them. Sauté mushrooms with a little minced garlic, toss into the leaves, add a slug of balsamic vinegar to the pan and reduce by half. Pour this over the leaves. Poached quail's or hen's eggs are an optional extra on top of the salad.

➤ An Eastern approach is to cook and drain spinach and dress it with an equal quantity of light soy sauce and sesame oil, sweetened with a little sugar, to which toasted ground or whole sesame seeds have been added.

➤ Make a salad of spinach leaves, Gorgonzola, walnuts and cooked green beans, and dress with sherry vinegar and walnut oil, with a hint of garlic.

➤ Stir-fry an assortment of vegetables: green beans, asparagus, broad beans, carrots, etc. and throw in young spinach leaves at the end. They will wilt instantly. Toss in some toasted, flaked almonds.

See also:

Spinach and Sesame Salad (page 90)
Haricot and French Beans with Champagne Butter Sauce (page 93)
Truffled Artichokes and New Potatoes (page 146)
Swiss Chard and Sorrel Tart (page 184)

Squashes & Pumpkins

It is only when you see gourds collectively that you can fully appreciate how weird and wonderful they are. The tenacious rambling vines with their huge fruits have the demeanour of some freakish prehistoric bird that cannot fly.

Gourd enthusiasm is catching on, and just recently supermarkets and greengrocers have started to sell an interesting variety over the year. It is not unusual to find celadon green 'Crown Prince' squashes, flame-orange 'Uchiki Kuri' pumpkins, and in my opinion the most magnificent, the 'Rouge Vif d'Etampes' pumpkins. And then of course there are others that you may be more familiar with, such as 'Little Gem' squashes and vegetable spaghetti.

The answer to the question 'When is a squash not a squash?' ought to be 'When it's a pumpkin', but Americans refer to pumpkins as winter squashes. They are all members of the Cucurbitae family, but the popular division of squashes into their season of maturity, summer or winter, is a woolly divide with considerable crossover.

A Ladybird guide for the cook is that summer squashes are courgette-like with soft flesh (spaghetti squash excepted), and winter squashes and pumpkins are long keepers with hard skins and a dense, smooth flesh which cooks beautifully; like apples you can store them through the winter. But, although they store well do not be misled – the fresher they are the better they eat; likewise do not get too excited by size.

Think in terms of yin and yang when cooking pumpkins and winter squashes: they are sufficiently austere to drip with wayward ingredients like cream, butter and cheese without becoming gratuitous. A soup that is no more than a pumpkin purée combined with cream and thinned to the correct consistency with stock, served with lots of grated Gruyère melting through it and little garlic croûtons, is every bit as gratifying as a really rich vichyssoise.

Pumpkins do not have the finesse of texture that squashes such as 'Rolet' and 'Butternut' do; a great deal of their flavour is contained in their juices which is why they are perfect for soup and purées. They also roast beautifully with olive oil or goosefat, some thyme, and sea salt.

Winter squashes and pumpkins have a chameleon quality: they are just as at home in a sweet puff-pastry tart flavoured with orange flower water as in a savoury gratin with porcini, served alongside roast game birds. As well as with spices like nutmeg, saffron and coriander, cinnamon and vanilla, they make successful marriages cooked with rosemary, thyme and sage, or some freshly chopped fines herbes or basil. Think eastwards too: root ginger and sesame are not out of place.

Spaghetti squash is unique. It was only when I came to make a mock rémoulade that I began to fully appreciate its qualities: effectively this is a fine julienne of a vegetable that would take any chef or cook considerable time to produce with a knife. Tasteless? Yes, to a degree, though delicate might be a kinder description, and delicate vegetables do have their uses – for one thing they are not going to upstage expensive ingredients like sole or halibut.

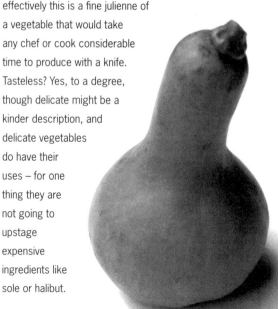

Gratin of Spaghetti Squash with Gruyère

A no-nonsense plateful of this is my idea of heaven. It also slots in nicely with a Sunday roast or as a more general accompaniment. I prefer to use Beaufort or Appenzeller rather than Gruyère, but they do take a little tracking down.

Bring a large pan of water to the boil. Prick the squash with a knife tip in places and cook, covered, for 25 minutes. When cool enough to handle, halve lengthwise and remove the seeds and spongy fibres. Run a fork along the length of the flesh and it will come away in strands; leave the mushy flesh immediately next to the skin. The strands should be on the firm side – they will soften when baked. Place the squash in a sieve and press out most of the additional juices.

Mix the cream, half the cheese, the kirsch and seasoning in a bowl and mix in the squash. Place in a gratin dish and scatter over the remaining cheese. You can prepare to this point in advance.

Heat the oven to 200°C fan oven/220°C or 425°F electric oven/Gas 7 and bake the gratin for 25–30 minutes, until golden in patches.

Serves 4 as a single dish,
6 as an accompaniment

1 spaghetti squash (approx. 1 kg/
    2 lb 4 oz)
150 ml/5 fl oz double cream
175 g/6 oz Gruyère, grated
1½ tablespoons kirsch
sea salt, freshly ground black pepper and
    nutmeg

Sweet and Sour Pumpkin

I learnt this recipe from a wonderful Pakistani cook called Samar Mazoor: a deliciously fragrant and sweet purée, sharpened with lime juice. This is a side dish – good with barbecued and grilled foods.

Should you happen to be feeling very energetic, you could skin the tomatoes, and if you happen to be feeling especially lazy you could use tinned ones.

Mix all the ingredients for the spice blend together. Heat the oil in a large saucepan, add the onion and fry until lightly golden. Add the garlic and stir, then the chopped tomato, pumpkin and spices and stir to mix. Add the water, bring to the boil, cover and simmer over a low heat for 20 minutes until the pumpkin is tender, giving it a stir half-way through.

Now add the honey and the lime juice. The mixture will probably still be quite wet, so turn the heat up and cook to reduce to a thick purée, making sure it does not catch. This will take about half an hour: adjust the salt at the very end.

Serves 4

6 tablespoons vegetable oil
1 onion, peeled and finely chopped
1 garlic clove, peeled and finely chopped
450 g/1 lb tomatoes, chopped
900 g/2 lb pumpkin (weight excluding
    skin and seeds), chopped
150 ml/5 fl oz water
1 tablespoon honey
1 tablespoon lime juice

Spice blend
¾ teaspoon sea salt
⅓ teaspoon cayenne pepper
⅓ teaspoon paprika
¼ teaspoon turmeric
1½ teaspoons ground cumin

Sauté of Butternut Squash, Red Pepper and Rocket with Eggs

This makes a delectable late breakfast or lunch: the general sound of sizzling and smell of squash frying draws spectators into the kitchen. This quantity is as much as you can make in a 25.5 cm/10 inch frying pan: use 2 pans if you double up.

Cut the skin off the squash. The easiest way to do this is to slice off the top and the base, then halve it so you have a neck and a dome and continue to cut the skin off each half. Quarter the dome and remove seeds and spongy fibres, then cut the flesh into 1 cm/½ inch dice. Peel, core and deseed the pepper and slice into strips.

Heat the olive oil in a 25.5 cm/10 inch frying pan over a medium heat. Add the squash, pepper and garlic simultaneously and season with salt, pepper and coriander. Cook for 15–20 minutes until the squash is soft in the centre and golden and caramelized on the outside, like sauté potatoes. While the squash is cooking make the croûtons.

Whisk the eggs in a bowl and season with salt and pepper. Toss the rocket into the squash to wilt; have your plates at the ready, turn the heat up high, tip in the eggs and turn with a spatula for 30–45 seconds until the egg is nearly set – serve it on the wet side. Scatter over the croûtons and eat straight away.

Photograph opposite page 176.

Serves 2–3

1 small 'Butternut' squash (650 g/
    1 lb 6 oz)
1 red pepper
2 tablespoons extra virgin olive oil
2 garlic cloves, peeled and minced
sea salt and freshly ground black pepper
¼ teaspoon coriander seeds, freshly
    ground
6 medium eggs
50 g/1¾ oz rocket, cut into 5 cm/
    2 inch lengths

Croûtons
1–2 slices sourdough or coarse white
    bread, cut in 1 cm/½ inch dice, fried
    in extra virgin olive oil

Other Ideas

➤ Make a soup by scooping out the seeds and fibres from the inside of a pumpkin and then filling it with grated Gruyère, cream, salt, pepper and nutmeg and baking in a hot oven until the flesh is tender: spoon out the inside, which is a delicious mass of creamy goo.

➤ Roast 'Butternut' squash along with other vegetables such as peppers, aubergine, onions and fennel. For a main course include chargrilled pieces of polenta.

➤ Include pumpkin as one of the vegetables in minestrone, instead of carrots.

➤ Make an Indian-style salad with cooked and cubed squash in Greek yoghurt, flavoured with a little ground cumin, with some chopped shallot.

➤ Make a frittata with sautéed squash and wild mushrooms: mix about 450 g/1 lb of cooked vegetables into 6 eggs beaten with 4 fl oz/¼ pint of double cream and a little Parmesan, and bake in a gratin dish for about 20 minutes in a fairly hot oven.

See also:

Escabeche with Thyme Toast (page 38)
Seven Vegetable Tagine (page 132)

Sweet Potatoes

Sweet potatoes are not in fact related to potatoes at all, but to the morning glory family. But since they look like potatoes and cook like potatoes and, indeed, are called potatoes, they have more than a little bit in common.

Well, they look quite like potatoes: elongated and with pointed ends, they come in colours ranging from brown to purplish red, with a flesh that can be ivory or a delicious shade of mandarin orange. It is the latter that are my favourites – by comparison to the pale-fleshed types they are especially sweet and succulent. The pale ones tend to be dry and mealy, quite chestnutty. And I usually try to buy largish ones, rather than slim ones. Apart from scraping away the skin to tell the colour of the flesh there is no sure way of determining it; the best thing is to ask.

Sweet potatoes will do most things that potatoes will do, although I have not tried them in a classic potato salad, but I see no reason why a fairly tart dressing should not work, with some chopped shallot or spring onion added. In the autumn and winter I like to bake them: as they emerge from the oven the skins should slip off quite easily, and if they have cooked long enough there will be a slick of caramel coating the flesh. Mash them up with butter, or smother with sour cream and coriander. Unlike ordinary baked potatoes, I am not so fond of eating the skin.

They seem to suit Eastern accents like garlic, ginger, chilli, lime juice and coriander, sesame oil and seeds. They are also good roasted; like pumpkins, they turn chewy and coloured at the edges rather than crisp.

Thai Coconut Soup with Roasted Sweet Potatoes

In the upstairs Mezzonine restaurant at Mezzo, Sir Terence Conran's restaurant in Soho, all the dishes are Malay-based, with Thai and a little Vietnamese thrown in. This arrives as a deep steaming bowlful of sweet and hot coconut soup; the original uses pumpkin, but sweet potato is just as good. If you have time, garnish the assembled bowls with finely sliced garlic and chilli, fried in a little oil, as shown in the photograph.

Preheat the oven to 200°C fan oven/220°C or 425°F electric oven/Gas 7. Peel the potatoes and cut into pieces 5 cm/2 inches long × 2.5 cm/1 inch thick. Place in a roasting tray, pour over a little oil, season and roast for 40–45 minutes.

Heat the chilli paste in a saucepan. Add the coconut milk, the milk, and the coconut cream, which will gradually dissolve, and bring to a simmer. Add the soy sauce and the sugar and season well with salt. This can be reheated.

Before the potato is done, bring a large pan of salted water to the boil and cook the fettucine, adding the beansprouts for the last 30 seconds to blanch them. Drain and arrange on the base of 4 soup bowls. Place the sweet potato on top. If necessary reheat the broth and pour over: scatter with coriander leaves.

Photograph between pages 176 and 177.

Serves 4–5

700 g/1 lb 9 oz orange-fleshed sweet
   potatoes (approx. 2 large or 3 smaller)
groundnut oil
sea salt and freshly ground black pepper
1 teaspoon chilli paste
2 × 400 ml/14 fl oz tins coconut milk
425 ml/¾ pint milk
70 g/2½ oz coconut cream
3 tablespoons light soy sauce
25 g/1 oz brown sugar
sea salt
175 g/6 oz fettucine or tagliatelle
110 g/4 oz beansprouts
3 tablespoons coriander leaves

Baked Sweet Potatoes with Ginger and Sesame Seeds

Preheat the oven to 160°C fan oven/170°C or 325°F electric oven/ Gas 3. Wash and dry the potatoes and bake them for 1½ hours. While they are cooking, heat some oil in a frying pan and cook the ginger until the strips are dry and beginning to colour; remove with a slotted spoon and drain on absorbent paper. Combine the sesame oil and soy sauce and reserve.

When the potatoes are cooked the skins should slip off easily. Thickly slice the flesh and arrange on a serving plate. Season with salt, pour the sesame-soy mixture over, and scatter over the sesame seeds and strips of ginger. Serve straight away.

Serves 4

900 g/2 lb orange-fleshed sweet
   potatoes
groundnut oil for frying
5 cm/2 inch piece of fresh ginger, skin
   removed and cut into fine squared
   strips
4 tablespoons light sesame oil (or 2
   tablespoons each of dark sesame oil
   and groundnut oil)
1 tablespoon light soy sauce
sea salt
1 heaped tablespoon sesame seeds,
   toasted

Sweet Potato Pancakes

These are wonderfully tender and puffed, and frying them in plenty of butter makes them nice and crisp at the edges. At a push you can reheat these, covered with foil, in a low oven, but try to eat them straight away.

Bring a pan of salted water to the boil. Peel and slice the sweet potatoes and cook for 7–8 minutes until tender. Drain and mash with the milk. Add the cream, flour, seasoning and nutmeg, and then, providing the mixture has cooled somewhat, add the egg yolks. Whisk the egg whites until stiff and fold into the batter.

Clarify the butter: melt it in a small saucepan, skim the surface foam and decant the clear yellow liquid, discarding the milk solids on the bottom. Heat a little clarified butter in 2 frying pans over a medium heat, and drop heaped tablespoons of the mixture into each one. They should spread to 7.5–10 cm/3–4 inches and be nice and thick – and you should be able to do about 6 pancakes at the same time. When the underside is golden and turning crisp at the edges, turn it and cook the other side. Remove to a plate and cook the remainder likewise.

Season the sour cream with the lemon juice, and serve the pancakes accompanied by the sour cream and the spring onions.

Serves 6 (makes 20)

500 g/1 lb 2 oz sweet potatoes (approx. 2 medium size)
125 ml/4 fl oz milk
50 ml/2 fl oz double cream
100 g/3½ oz flour, sieved
sea salt and freshly ground black pepper
freshly grated nutmeg
3 medium eggs, separated
70 g/2½ oz unsalted butter

To serve
150 ml/5 fl oz sour cream
squeeze of lemon juice
4 heaped tablespoons finely sliced spring onions

Other Ideas

➤ Make bubble and squeak or colcannon using sweet potatoes instead of ordinary ones.

➤ Make a classic gratin, using sweet potatoes, double cream and freshly grated nutmeg.

➤ Make sweet potato cakes by mixing mashed sweet potato with chopped shallots, parsley and egg and frying them.

➤ Make a sweet potato and spinach soup and serve with a spoon of crème fraîche flavoured with lime juice.

➤ Make a purée of a mixture of root vegetables, including sweet potatoes, parsnip, turnip and celeriac.

Sauté of Butternut Squash, Red Pepper and Rocket with Eggs (page 170)

Thai Coconut Soup with Roasted Sweet Potatoes (page 173)

Sweetcorn with Chilli-soy Butter (page 180)

Sweetcorn

It was a visit to Fetzer Valley Oaks in California that altered my perception of corn, or maize. There was a greenhouse with a long wooden table in it, and neatly arranged like soldiers in rows were dried heads of corn, sheathed in their parchment-like husks. Working our way down the row, we selected heads at random, pulling back the husks and the silk. Every one was a different configuration of colours, ranging from white to pale yellow, bright yellow, crimson, purple, black, and the most stunning marbled kernels. These in fact were destined for decoration and not the table.

Maguelonne Toussaint-Samat, in *History of Food*, tells a charming story explaining these colours. The Zuni Indians say that once their ancestors the Ashiwis lived underground. There was a very beautiful group of young girls who had never been seen in daylight, so their beauty went unnoticed. One day the Ashiwis emerged overground, and two sorcerers met the girls and asked who they were. 'We are the maidens of the maize.' 'Where are your ears?' the sorcerers asked. The girls said they had lost them. So the sorcerers struck the ground; up sprang six plants, each with a different coloured ear corresponding to the six emblematic colours of the six regions of New Mexico.

The different pigments exist in different locations of the kernels. The reddy, purple hues lie in a thin, peripheral layer, whereas the yellow coloration is in the endosperm, which forms the basis of cornmeal – this is always yellow and never coloured.

Of the many variants of corn, the one that is familiar to us as a vegetable is 'sweetcorn', which has a high sugar content. Roger Phillips, author of many botanical books including the full colour encyclopedia *Vegetables*, reports that in America (where they are big on their corn) it is graded according to the colour of the grain, whether it is yellow, white, blue or a combination, and on how sweet it is: 'supersweet', 'extra sweet' and 'sugary enhanced'.

Corn was a Native American staple, and grew in conjunction with beans and squashes, or gourds, forming a naturally symbiotic relationship. This impressed the colonists, who in their ignorance of how to include it in their diet contracted pellagra, a disease caused by protein and niacin deficiency that results when maize is the main source of food. There seems to be some justice in this, considering the fashion in which the colonists abused Native American hospitality.

Sweetcorn is true to its name: it is sweet, and this needs balancing out. Hot and spicy Thai flavours suit it well, and herbs like coriander and lemon grass. Barbecuing it works wonders. It is also quite rich in itself and responds to sharp, acidic dressings and sauces. As a purée it will always be textured and you may prefer to sieve it.

The ubiquitous baby corn is not to my personal taste – it offers little that the mature cobs do in flavour or texture, and unless it is chargrilled it has an unpleasant ammoniacal savour.

Preparation

There is a variety of paraphernalia for preparing and eating sweetcorn, such as a special American grater for removing kernels from the cob (I usually use a sharp knife). They also go in for desilking brushes. These too I can live without. Then of course there are all those dinky designed corn prongs for sticking in each end of a cob to save you getting your hands hot and sticky. In my mind hot, sticky and dripping with butter is all part of the fun when eating corn. I prefer to simply wait until it cools down enough to hold it.

Cooking

The sugar in sweetcorn starts to convert to starch as soon as it is picked, which is why cooking lore has it that the way to eat corn-

Tomatoes Flambéed in Pastis, with Fennel and Feta (page 191)

on-the-cob is to have a pan of water on the boil, go into the field, harvest your cobs, run back to the kitchen with them, and cook them. One has to take into account that modern varieties have been developed to allow for a loss of sugar by the time the consumer comes to pick them. Having boiled corn-on-the-cob in salted and in sugared water as is sometimes suggested, the sugared water produced an unpalatably sweet cob.

To cook corn-on-the-cob, bring a large pan of salted water to the boil. Pull back and cut off the husks, pull off the silk, and boil the cobs for 15 minutes. Remove and serve straight away with butter sauce, such as those suggested in Other Ideas.

Should you want sweetcorn kernels off the cob, it is quite easy to strip the kernels with a large sharp knife. Stand the cob upright on a chopping board and cut downwards, working around the cob; several strokes will do it.

Tamales

There was a time during the 1980s when Mexican tamales were de rigueur on Californian menus, and to some extent they filtered over here too, but never really took off. They're like a dumpling that's been steamed inside a casing of corn sheaths, and the finest achieve a delicate, sweet flavour and a light and fluffy texture. They're delicious eaten with lively sauces or smothered with melted cheese.

On a visit to San Francisco I ate genuine tamales, and after lunch managed to beg a few minutes' observation in the kitchen to see how they were made. It soon became clear to me why proper tamales are virtually impossible to produce at home. To start at the beginning, the corn is left to dry on the stalk, then harvested. To prepare the *masa* (dough used to make tortillas), the whole dried *hominy* (dried corn kernels) is boiled with water and with lime, which softens the kernel. The outer skin is then removed, and the remainder is ground wet into a dough, though it can also be dried and sieved to produce a flour which is supposed to make lighter tamales.

To assemble the tamales, dried-out corn husks are soaked in boiling water for 30 minutes. These are spread with some of the tamale dough, then a filling, and loosely packaged up and tied with a long strip of husk so they are watertight – if water enters they will be soggy.

Next a steamer is lined with more corn husks and the tamales are quite tightly packed into it. The lid is sealed with a damp cloth to prevent any steam from escaping, and the tamales are cooked for about 3 hours. The water must not go off the boil, but can be topped up as necessary. Once cooked the tamales should be comparatively spongy, and light. They can be reheated in an oven or over a low griddle.

In Mexico you can buy a ready ground *masa* mix, but I have not come across it here – the husks can occasionally be found and you can obviously make your own. If you do fancy trying your hand, while they are a long way from being authentic, polenta produces very nice tamales, infused with the fragrance of the corn husk.

Thai Sweetcorn Fritters with a Dipping Sauce

Place the water, butter, sugar and corn in a small saucepan. Bring to a simmer, cover and cook for 15 minutes or until tender, then stir in the salt. Make the batter by whisking the egg yolk with the flour, oil and water. Allow this to stand for 20 minutes.

While the batter is resting, make the dipping sauce. Simmer the vinegar, sugar and salt together in a small saucepan until they are reduced by half, pour over the garlic and chilli and leave to cool.

Whisk the egg white until stiff and fold it into the batter, then stir in the corn kernels, the coriander and the lemon grass. Heat plenty of groundnut oil in a wok or a pan to 190°C/375°F. Drop tablespoons of the fritter mixture into the oil and cook until golden on the underside, then turn and cook the other side. Remove the fritters with a slotted utensil and drain on kitchen paper while you cook the remainder, allowing the oil to come back up to temperature with each batch. Serve the fritters straight away, dipping them into a central bowl of the sauce.

Serves 4

Corn
175 ml/6 fl oz water
25 g/1 oz unsalted butter
½ teaspoon sugar
250 g/9 oz corn kernels (approx. 2 cobs)
1 level teaspoon sea salt

Batter
1 medium egg, separated
60 g/2 oz plain flour
1 tablespoon olive oil
50 ml/2 fl oz water
2 tablespoons finely chopped coriander
2 teaspoons finely chopped lemon grass
groundnut oil for deep-frying

Dipping sauce
175 ml/6 fl oz rice wine or white wine vinegar
30 g/1¼ oz caster sugar
⅓ teaspoon sea salt
2 garlic cloves, peeled and finely sliced
1 level teaspoon finely sliced red chilli

Sweetcorn with Chilli-soy Butter

Bring a large pan of water to the boil. Slice off the base of each cob and pull off the outer husks and silk, and cut a slice off the top. Add the cobs to the pan, bring back to the boil, half cover with a lid and cook for 15–20 minutes until tender, then drain.

While the cobs are cooking, melt the butter in a saucepan, add the chilli to the butter and leave to infuse. Reheat the butter, stir in the soy sauce and coriander and serve it poured over the corn.

Photograph between pages 176 and 177.

Serves 4

4 corn-on-the-cob
175 g/6 oz unsalted butter
1 teaspoon finely chopped red chilli
1 tablespoon light soy sauce
1 heaped tablespoon finely chopped
   coriander

Fast

Corn and Vanilla Ice-cream

Until I met Sirio Maccioni, owner of New York's Le Cirque restaurant, my reaction to sweetcorn ice-cream would have been thanks, but no thanks. But having tasted the finest crème brûlée ever at his hands, served warm rather than chilled, I think he could persuade me to try virtually any flavour.

Thinking about it, corn ice-cream does ring with a certain gastronomic good sense — think of all those lovely polenta cakes, and sweet muffins. This ice-cream has a beautiful freshness to it, and a really rich, heavy texture which is very pleasant.

It is nicest served freshly churned; you can make the mix in advance, keep it refrigerated and churn it just before you need it. Obviously it can be frozen, but remember that ice-cream is not a long keeper, so try to use it within hours of making it, and do not keep it for longer than 2 days.

The corn kernels should be freshly stripped from the cob, by holding the cob upright on the chopping board and cutting down with a large, sharp knife. Place these in a small saucepan with the milk and sugar, bring to the boil, cover and simmer over a low heat for 15 minutes. Purée and pass through a sieve into a bowl.

Whisk the corn purée with the cream, vanilla seeds, eggs and Cointreau and pass through a sieve. Freeze in your ice-cream maker according to the manufacturer's instructions. Remove to a bowl, cover and freeze.

Serves 4

285 g/10 oz raw corn kernels
  (1½–2 cobs)
225 ml/8 fl oz milk
125 g/4½ oz caster sugar
350 ml/12 fl oz double cream
seeds of 1 vanilla pod
2 medium eggs, whisked
1 tablespoon Cointreau

Other Ideas

➤ Make a cream of sweetcorn soup and serve it with sour cream, finely sliced spring onions and chopped coriander.

➤ Vary the butter for corn-on-the-cob by flavouring it with freshly ground nutmeg, roasted and ground cumin or coriander, or freshly chopped herbs such as parsley, coriander, or fines herbes.

➤ Make a sweetcorn salsa with cooked corn kernels, roasted, skinned and diced red pepper, chopped onion or shallot, lime juice, chilli and coriander.

➤ Make a proper 'creamed corn' by simmering cooked kernels with double cream, seasoning and nutmeg until they are coated in a reduced, thickened cream sauce. Sprinkle with chopped flat-leaved parsley.

➤ For barbecuing, you need cobs with all their outer husks intact: peel these back and pull off the silk, then tie the leaves back in place with string. Soak them in a sink or bucket of cold water for 30 minutes, then barbecue.

Swiss Chard

The French, Italians and Spanish are far more loyal to Swiss chard than we are, and it grows very well in this country so there's no excuse. Sadly, though, it is limited to a few enlightened greengrocers and gardeners.

While it is a beet, it is the swollen leaf stalks we prize rather than the roots. In an ideal world it is not only the common green and white variety we should have access to, but 'Rhubarb Chard' as well, which sports dramatic crumpled green leaves, and the even more dramatic 'Rainbow Chard' which has yellow, orange and red stalks.

I like Swiss chard best when it is married with robust flavours like anchovies, garlic, chilli, porcini and capers, or dipped into a thick, yellow glob of aïoli along with the usual cold vegetables. The Lebanese smother it with tahini sauce and sprinkle it with mint, and the Italians use the leaf as an alternative to spinach for blending with ricotta and filling ravioli.

Perhaps the final word should go to that *éminence grise* John Evelyn, author of *Acetaria*, who cooked the leaves in their own juices and served them on buttered toast – maybe from time to time he treated himself to a lightly poached egg on top.

Preparation

Basically Swiss chard is two vegetables in one: the fleshy midribs or chards can be treated like seakale, and the leaves cooked and eaten like spinach. They do in any case need separating, since they require different cooking times.

Wrapped in clingfilm and stored in the bottom of the fridge, chard will keep for about 2 days, but it has a tendency to go limp quite quickly.

Cut off the root of the vegetable to separate the stalks, and discard any damaged ribs or leaves, then slice the green leaf part off the midrib and wash the leaves and midribs separately in water.

Cooking

In character Swiss chard leaf is more hefty than spinach; it does not collapse in quite such a dramatic fashion.

To cook the leaf part, bring a large pan of salted water to the boil, slice the leaves and add them to the pan, bring the water back to the boil and cook for 2 minutes. Drain and refresh the leaves in a sink of cold water. Now squeeze out the moisture between your hands, so you have balls of cooked vegetable. These can be treated as you would cooked spinach: reheat them with a knob of butter in a frying pan when required, or blend them into fillings and so forth.

To cook the midribs, either steam them whole until they are tender and then slice them into thin lengths, or slice them thinly across the midrib before cooking, in which case work quickly to avoid discoloration. Heat some butter or olive oil in a frying pan, add the chopped chard and a generous squeeze of lemon juice, season and sauté until it begins to give out its juices, cover with a lid and let it steam for 3 minutes.

Swiss Chard and Sorrel Tart

This is based on a recipe in *Lulu's Provençal Table* by Richard Olney. If you are going to serve it cold, halve the number of eggs for a creamier set.

Preheat the oven to 180°C fan oven/190°C or 375°F electric oven/Gas 5. Roll the pastry 0.25 cm/⅛ inch thick on a lightly floured surface and line a 25.5 × 5 cm/10 × 2 inch tart tin so the pastry hangs over the sides of the tin. Weight with foil and baking beans (dried pulses will do) so the sides are well secured. Bake for 25 minutes until lightly golden, then remove the foil and beans.

While the pastry is baking, bring a large pan of salted water to the boil. Heat the olive oil in a largish saucepan and sweat the onion and garlic over a low heat for 10–15 minutes until slippery and soft, stirring occasionally. Add the sorrel and cook until it turns a dull khaki.

Add the chard and spinach leaves to the boiling water, bring back to the boil and cook for 2 minutes. Drain, refresh in cold water, squeeze out thoroughly and chop. Add these leaves to the onion and garlic and cook for about 10 minutes, seasoning well.

Whisk the eggs and cream in a large bowl. Add the chard mixture, stir well to blend, and pour into the tart case. Sprinkle over the grated Parmesan and bake for 30–35 minutes. Trim the pastry either in line with the top of the tin, or with the top of the filling. Serve about 10 minutes out of the oven rather than piping hot.

Serves 6

250 g/9 oz ready-made puff pastry
4 tablespoons extra virgin olive oil
1 large onion, peeled, halved and sliced
1 head of garlic, peeled and sliced
225 g/8 oz sorrel, ribs removed, and sliced
450 g/1 lb Swiss chard, leaf part only
225 g/8 oz spinach
sea salt and freshly ground black pepper
4 medium eggs
300 ml/½ pint double cream
3 tablespoons freshly grated Parmesan

Chard Midribs with Soft Boiled Eggs

This makes a very easy supper. I have always liked asparagus in this role, and Swiss chard ribs are equally good.

Bring a large pan of water to the boil and acidulate the water with the lemon juice. Tidy the ribs and cut them into strips several inches long and about 1 cm/½ inch wide. Add them to the pan, bring back to the boil, and add the eggs. Cook the eggs for 6 minutes, by which time the chard should also be tender.

Drain the two and toss the ribs in the saucepan with the butter and seasoning. Serve beside the eggs with the Parmesan separately; dip them in the yolk and sprinkle with a little cheese as you go. Accompany with toast.

Serves 2

juice of ½ lemon
350 g/12 oz Swiss chard ribs
4 medium eggs
15 g/½ oz unsalted butter
sea salt and freshly ground black pepper
2 teaspoons freshly grated Parmesan

To serve
buttered brown toast

Creamed Salad of Chard Leaf

This is half-way between a tartare sauce and a salad, deliciously rich and flavoured with gherkins and tarragon: serve a heaped tablespoon beside grilled or fried white fish, or with vegetables dipped in batter and deep-fried, or simply as an appetizer by way of a dip.

It is the chard leaf you require, but a small amount of the stalk tapers into the leaf section and it is fine to include this.

Bring a large pan of salted water to the boil. Wash and slice the chard, add to the pan, bring back to the boil and cook for 2 minutes. Drain and refresh in cold water, then squeeze out excess water.

Whisk the egg yolk with the mustard in a bowl, then slowly whisk in the oil to make a mayonnaise until the mixture is very thick. Stir in the gherkin and tarragon.

Place the cooked and squeezed-out chard on a chopping board and chop finely. Stir this into the mayonnaise, and adjust the salt. Keep covered in the fridge until required.

Serves 3–4

---

leaf part of 1 head of chard that is
    approx. 1 kg/2 lb 4 oz total weight
1 medium egg yolk
½ teaspoon Dijon mustard
150–200 ml/5–7 fl oz groundnut oil
1 heaped tablespoon finely chopped
    gherkin
5 tarragon leaves, finely chopped
sea salt

Other Ideas

➤ Steam the midribs, layer them with grated Parmesan and melted butter in a gratin dish, and bake until the surface cheese is melted and golden.

➤ Cook the leaf part of Swiss chard and make a salad, dressing it with extra virgin olive oil, balsamic vinegar, salt and freshly ground black pepper.

➤ Make a pie filling by blending the leaf part of the chard with ricotta or feta cheese, and roasted red peppers. Line a cake or tart tin with layers of buttered filo pastry and put in the filling. Enclose the pie with the overhanging pastry, butter it copiously and bake until golden and crisp.

➤ Sauté the cooked leaves with pine-nuts and raisins.

➤ Steam the midribs and serve them with brown butter, capers and toasted almonds.

➤ Steam the midribs, paint them with olive oil, chargrill and serve them with shavings of Parmesan.

Tomatoes

While we may not have access to the type of sensual Mediterranean pleasure of picking a fresh fig in the early morning sun and eating it, we are at least able in late summer to walk around the garden eating tomatoes straight from the vine, at their sweetest having ripened fully in the sun out of doors.

Tomato flavour can be affected by many variables – these can include how they are grown and the type of soil, as well as the weather. It is no old wives' tale that they enjoy neglect: overfed and overwatered tomatoes will be lacking in flavour – they thrive on stress.

In *Sicilian Food*, Mary Taylor Simeti notes that the harvesting of tomatoes begins in July, and those grown around Alcamo, known as *siccanis*, are grown dry on unirrigated land. If it has been a particularly dry spring, they may only have received a few ladles of water in June, 'yet produce intensely flavoured tomatoes dripping copious amounts of juice'.

It is hard to imagine Italian food before the arrival of tomatoes in Europe in the sixteenth century. A half-hardy plant native to Peru and Mexico, the tomato was introduced by the Spanish as an ornamental greenhouse climber. At first it was known as the love apple; our name derives from the Mexican *tomatl*.

'Pixie', 'Pink Panther', 'Tigerella' and 'Golden Boy' collectively sound more like racehorses than a vibrant collection of fruits. Red and orange, yellow, pink and striped, tomatoes can be ribbed, square, tiny like currants or pear-shaped. Most cooks today are familiar with marmande or beefsteak tomatoes, plum and cherry as well as the standard round varieties. Tomatoes 'grown for flavour' has been one of the more absurd marketing ploys of recent years. And sadly, those advertised as being vine-ripened also come in for abuse, often having been picked too early. But there are good tomatoes on the market too, the thing being to experiment and locate a good supply locally, and keep going back.

Selection

Tomatoes should have a balance of sugar and acidity; without that sourness they can taste very bland, and without the sweetness they will be too tart. Buy tomatoes which are firm, with a smooth, taut skin. And the skin should not be too thick and tough, just as the texture of the tomato flesh should be tender and succulent and not dry.

While Britain is capable of producing delicious tomatoes, unfortunately the greater percentage produced by large commercial nurseries are grown indoors under glass with a reliance on chemicals, and a view to long shelf-life and uniformity of appearance. Apart from being coddled, they are usually picked early before they have fully ripened and developed their flavour. French and Italian tomatoes grown outdoors make a better purchase during the summer.

Skinned and diced tomato

There are numerous occasions when just a spoon or two of skinned and diced tomato (concassée) will enliven a dish – add it raw to a salad when you dress it, or stir it into a sauce or pasta, at the end if you want to add a fresh accent, and at the beginning if you want it to blend in with the sauce.

The marmande or beefsteak varieties are best for this. Cut out a small cone of flesh to remove the core and cut a small cross on the base. Dip into boiling water for 20–30 seconds, then plunge them immediately into cold water and slip off the skin. Quarter and scoop out the seeds. Dice the flesh.

Passata

In Sicily the bulk of the summer crop of tomatoes is turned into sauce for the winter. A friend, Ninny Ravida, who prepares gallons

of tomato sauce each summer, first squeezes the tomatoes to provide juice, then cooks them for about 1 hour. Next she sweats some shallots or onions, adds the cooked tomatoes and continues cooking until the sauce is a dense cream. It is then sieved and bottled in soft drink or beer bottles.

You cannot even begin to compare bottled shop-bought passata with this in terms of quality, but it is the closest we have in terms of convenience.

Tomato extract

The grocer's stalls in the market in Palermo, Sicily, have mounds of thick crimson paste which they sell in small blocks. This is *u 'strattu*, a sun-dried tomato extract with a unique and rich flavour. You can buy it from Carluccio's, 28a Neal Street, London WC1, and it keeps almost indefinitely.

I now keep a small jar of this in my fridge, the surface sealed with a film of olive oil. It needs to be reconstituted before it is used, either by simmering in a sauce or covering it with boiling water and letting it relax into a purée. In its absence, of course, you can substitute an ordinary tomato paste – its uses are the same although it has a more pronounced flavour. It is good used in conjunction with fresh tomatoes to provide a more rounded sauce.

Cooking

I use three seasonings with tomatoes: salt, pepper and sugar, just a pinch of which will bring out the flavour. For a plain tomato salad, I skin the tomatoes, slice them, season them with salt, pepper and sugar, and leave them until the juices start running, for about 15 minutes. If I want an instant tomato salad, or if I am going on a picnic, I often serve them plain like this without any oil.

If you are cooking with tomatoes, a soup for instance, it is a good idea to include the skins and sieve the contents after cooking, as they will enhance both the colour and the flavour.

Plum Tomatoes with a Herb Crust

A very classical side dish: halved tomatoes grilled with breadcrumbs, Gruyère and parsley. For a vegetarian meal you could use the same crust for mushrooms and courgettes, hence serving a selection – but bake rather than grill these.

Cut the tops off the tomatoes to remove the cores and halve them lengthwise. Lay them out on a baking tray cut side up. Blend together all the remaining ingredients in a bowl and press as a crust on to each tomato half.

Heat the grill on medium low and grill the tomatoes until the crust is golden and the tomato cooked. If your grill only has one setting, cook the tomatoes at a distance from the filament – they will take around 20 minutes.

Serves 4

9 plum tomatoes
85 g/3 oz white breadcrumbs
60 g/2 oz grated Gruyère
60 g/2 oz unsalted butter
3 tablespoons chopped parsley
½ teaspoon Dijon mustard
1 level teaspoon thyme
sea salt and freshly ground black pepper

Tomatoes Flambéed in Pastis, with Fennel and Feta

This little dish finds its roots with a recipe in Guy Savoy's *Vegetable Magic*. It is nicest served with crusty white bread either as a first course or a lunch dish: there are plenty of juices for mopping. Do not worry too much about the flambéeing of the tomatoes – pastis does not flare up as dramatically as brandy. In fact the sight of the halved, baked red tomatoes licked by the blue of the flames is incredibly pretty.

Preheat the oven to 180°C fan oven/190°C or 375°F electric oven/ Gas 5. Halve 400 g/14 oz of the tomatoes horizontally and place on a baking sheet. Season, drizzle over 2 teaspoons of the olive oil, and bake for 7–8 minutes. Meanwhile reduce the remainder of the tomatoes to a purée in a food processor, then pass through a sieve into a bowl.

Remove shoots from the fennel bulb, halve vertically cutting through the shoots and slice into strips. Heat the remaining oil in a small saucepan and sweat the fennel for 3–4 minutes, then add the tomato sauce, season, and simmer for another 7–8 minutes until the fennel is soft and coated in a thick sauce.

When the baked tomatoes are removed from the oven, warm the pastis in a ladle over a gas flame, or in a small saucepan, ignite it and gradually pour over the tomatoes. When the flames subside, pour the residual liquor into the fennel and tomato mixture. Place this in the base of a baking dish with the baked tomatoes on top, then cover with the feta slices. You can prepare the dish to this point in advance.

Return the dish to the oven for 3–5 minutes to warm through, and serve scattered with the olives and parsley, with a little more olive oil drizzled over.

Photograph opposite page 177.

Serves 4

700 g/1 lb 9 oz small tomatoes
sea salt and freshly ground black pepper
2 tablespoons extra virgin olive oil
1 fennel bulb
50 ml/2 fl oz pastis (e.g. Pernod)
175 g/6 oz feta cheese, sliced
60 g/2 oz black olives, pitted
1 heaped tablespoon chopped flat-leaved
    parsley

To serve
extra virgin olive oil

Gazpacho

This is a very flavourful and quite rich gazpacho – you don't need it by the bucketful. The main point is to use really sweet tomatoes; if you can't get cherry then some other small variety, vine-ripened, can be good. As well as the suggested garnishes, little diced croûtons are always appreciated, and sliced tiger prawns or lobster for a special occasion.

Place all the ingredients for the soup in a blender and reduce to a purée, then pass through a sieve: you will have to do this in batches. Chill for at least 1 hour, and don't keep for longer than is necessary.

Serve with a garnish of avocado, a few strips of basil and some olive oil splashed over each bowl, or use sliced tiger prawns instead of the avocado. Or both, of course, and a few croûtons thrown in.

Serves 4

1.35 kg/2½ lb cherry tomatoes
1 cucumber, peeled
1 clove of garlic, peeled and chopped
1 heaped teaspoon finely chopped fresh
   red chilli
2 heaped teaspoons chopped onion
300 ml/½ pint extra virgin olive oil
1 tablespoon red wine or sherry vinegar
2 heaped teaspoons caster sugar
2 rounded teaspoons sea salt
freshly ground black pepper

Garnish
½ avocado, sliced
a few basil leaves cut into thin strips
extra virgin olive oil

Other Ideas

➤ At the height of their season during the summer when tomatoes are sweet and very ripe, you can make the simplest of soups by blitzing them in a food processor with salt, pepper, a pinch of sugar and a couple of basil leaves. Pass through a sieve and serve cold.

➤ Make an uncooked tomato sauce for macaroni with skinned and diced tomato, extra virgin olive oil, salt, pepper and shredded basil: warm through in a saucepan to just above blood temperature and then dress the pasta. You could also mix it plentifully with cooked pasta shells to serve as a salad.

➤ Red and yellow cherry and pear tomatoes make delicious crudités with creamy dips laced with herbs; or with tapenade. Serve a mixture of vegetables including radishes, fennel and carrots.

➤ The best bruschetta I have ever eaten was in a hilltop village in Tuscany and was clearly devised to use up the day-before's bread. Toasted and wet with olive oil, it was spread with really over-ripe mushy tomatoes, first skinned and then pounded, and left to seep into the toast so it was nice and soggy.

➤ Bruschetta is a variation on the theme of tomatoes on toast, my favourite breakfast as a child. The toast needs to be well-buttered and crisp, and the tomatoes either grilled or roasted in the oven.

➤ Marcella Hazan's 'simplest and freshest of all tomato sauces' is perfect for spaghetti, lasagne and gnocchi.

Take a kilo (approx. 2 lb) of fresh, ripe plum tomatoes, wash, cut in half lengthways and simmer in a covered saucepan for 10 minutes. Purée through a mouli-légumes back into the pan. Add 100 g (about 4 oz) of butter, 1 onion, peeled and halved, ¼ teaspoon of sugar and a little salt, and cook at a slow but steady simmer for 45 minutes. Adjust the salt and discard the onion.

See also:

Watercress

Why is it that watercress, now with us twelve months of the year, has been all but relegated to the waxworks, while rocket is labelled on menus like a precious designer frock? Between the two, I have a preference for watercress – nothing can match that uniquely squeaky pepperiness.

Watercress is a semi-aquatic herb, and grows wild in British lowlands, in streams and ditches where there is running water. I cannot advise collecting it in the wild, however, because of the risk of liver fluke, spread by cattle and sheep.

To cultivate it is something of an art; as with so many foods, there is watercress and there is watercress, and not all methods of cultivation and handling do the end product justice. Hampshire is the area famous for its watercress, around the Test and Itchen valleys, which have chalk springs. On visiting an organic watercress farm in Hill Deverill, the first impression was the wet. You are never far from the rippling of pure spring water pumped up from 120 feet below the ground, running at a constant 11°C. This may sound chilly by summer swimming standards, but during the winter it acts as an inbuilt hot water bottle for the watercress plants. The beds are elegant and elongated, lawns of glossy, cushioned clumps, plants about 23 cm/9 inches tall when mature, anchored by a complex system of fine white rootlets to the gravel bed below. And below the beds is a complex system of sluice gates which open and close to let water in and out, draining and flooding, with half a million gallons passing through each acre every day.

It was not so long ago that watercress was a seasonal crop, coming on to the market in September and petering out in May when it flowered, hence thriving at a time of the year when lettuces and other salad leaves were scarce. One way around this seasonal limitation has been to cultivate a late-flowering variety, which, within a carefully controlled procedure, can be coaxed into producing all year round. This means we are lucky enough to have it in the summer.

For other growers the solution has been to keep replanting with

seedlings. But it is questionable whether this is an ideal solution for the consumer; because these flower quickly and are therefore harvested young, they do not have the flavour that the mature plants offer.

As most watercress eaters know, watercress comes in two varieties: prepacked and bunched. Now, do not be fooled. The prepack may present itself as an offer to appease the cook, making your lot that much easier, with no messy roots to cut off and no need for washing, but you are also buying convenience at the expense of flavour. What a bunch of watercress guarantees is that the plants have grown to a certain height, and therefore have maturity and capture the natural peppery taste.

If watercress loves water, it also loves ice. Packing it on to the stalks to allow ice cold water to percolate through the pack may be a method that predates motor transport as far as supermarkets are concerned, but it is essential to prevent the watercress from drying out.

Once upon a time watercress sandwiches were a traditional Sunday night tea, especially in the north in mining communities. Personally I could eat one every day: a really fresh white roll spread with unsalted butter and crammed with watercress so that it spills out at the sides, with the occasional slice of smoked salmon or runny Brie in with it.

Selection

When buying watercress, appearance will tell you almost everything you need to know: it should have beautiful, blemish-free, plump, green, peppery leaves, and succulent stems. Anything on the point of wilting or discolouring is past its best.

Preparation

Even when watercress advertises that it has been washed, I prefer to refresh it in a sink of very cold water. If the weather is hot, it is not a bad idea to give it a soak to perk it up. Remove and discard any tough stalks.

It is worth remembering that watercress and rocket are interchangeable in most dishes. Watercress plays an obvious role in salads, and because of its character is a useful leaf for partnering with other characterful ingredients – walnuts, pecans or pinenuts, blue cheeses, Emmental or feta, black olives and the like.

Cooking

Cooked? Well a chilled watercress soup is hard to beat, and the secret there, as well as for sauces, is merely to blanch it – this will preserve the chlorophyll and the flavour, so prepare your soup or sauce base and add the watercress at the last minute. It is excellent wilted in butter, and can then be used with pasta, to fill an omelette, or just thrown into a stir-fry at the end.

Poached Eggs with Watercress Sauce

A very easy dish to throw together for lunch, with some bread.

Bring a large pan of salted water to the boil. Pick out any tough stalks from the watercress and blanch it for 30 seconds. Using a slotted spoon, remove the watercress to a sieve and refresh under cold running water: press out the excess. Bring the cream to a boil in a small saucepan, pour into a liquidizer, add the watercress and stock, liquidize, and pass through a sieve back into the cream saucepan. Reheat, and add the Parmesan and seasoning. The sauce should have a coating consistency.

Bring the pan of water back to the boil and acidulate it with the vinegar. Stir the water into a lazy whirlpool. Break the eggs one at a time into the water. Once they rise to the surface, trim the ragged tails of white and cook a couple of minutes longer. They should cook about 4 minutes in all, just set on the outside of the yolk and runny within: you will need to do this in 2 lots. Remove with a slotted utensil and drain thoroughly. Serve 2 per person, coated with the sauce.

Serves 4

white wine vinegar for acidulating water
8 medium eggs

Sauce
225 g/8 oz watercress
200 ml/7 fl oz double cream
100 ml/3½ fl oz vegetable stock
2 heaped tablespoons freshly grated
    Parmesan
sea salt and freshly ground black pepper

Watercress and Ricotta Cheesecake

This is half-way between a mousse and a quiche. It's very luxurious and quite rich, so serve it with a salad, something like frisée, walnut and avocado. It will serve as a starter or a main course.

Preheat the oven to 170°C fan oven/180°C or 350°F electric oven/Gas 4. To prepare the base, grease a 20.5 cm/8 inch springform cake tin with the butter, using all of it. Season the breadcrumbs with salt and cayenne pepper and press them on to the base and sides of the tin.

To make the filling, place the cream and watercress in a saucepan and bring to the boil. Take off the heat and cool somewhat. Place all the ingredients for the filling in a liquidizer and purée. Carefully pour the mixture into the prepared tin so as not to disturb the breadcrumbs, and bake for 50–60 minutes until lightly golden and set. Allow to cool – as the cheesecake contracts, the breadcrumb lining comes away from the sides so it does not crack. Cover and chill.

Serves 6

Crust
25 g/1 oz unsalted butter, softened
sea salt and cayenne pepper
5 tablespoons fresh white breadcrumbs

Filling
300 ml/½ pint double cream
175 g/6 oz watercress, coarsely
  chopped
3 medium eggs
250 g/9 oz ricotta
½ small garlic clove
sea salt, freshly ground black pepper and
  nutmeg
40 g/1½ oz freshly grated Parmesan

Salad of Watercress, Stilton, Pears and Walnuts

A salad in which all the ingredients are destined for each other: a touch salty, a touch sweet, with peppery leaves of watercress and aromatic walnut oil.

Mix the vinegar with the seasoning, then add the oil.

Slice the Stilton. Peel, quarter and core the pears, and cut into long thin slices. Dress the watercress with the vinaigrette, mix in the other ingredients and serve immediately.

Serves 4

Dressing
1 teaspoon sherry vinegar
sea salt and freshly ground black pepper
2 tablespoons walnut oil

Salad
175 g/6 oz ripe Stilton, excluding rind
400 g/14 oz ripe pears (2 large)
60 g/2 oz watercress
60 g/2 oz walnut pieces

Other Ideas

➤ Make a salad with watercress, Emmental and pecan nuts, and dress it with a nut vinaigrette. Beetroot, walnuts and feta is another good mix.

➤ Another salad: watercress and blanched cauliflower dressed with a lemon and anchovy vinaigrette.

➤ Dress warm borlotti or cannellini beans with olive oil, lemon zest and chopped shallots, and toss in lots of watercress. Serve on toast rubbed with garlic and drizzled with olive oil.

➤ Make a watercress soup by sweating 300 g/10½ oz of watercress in a knob of butter, adding 1 finely sliced potato and 1.2 litres/2 pints of boiling water. Simmer for 6 minutes, then liquidize. Good with a swirl of cream and croûtons.

➤ Make a creamy watercress sauce for baby pasta shells by sweating chopped shallots and lots of watercress in a little butter, adding a slug of wine and reducing it, then adding cream, simmering for a few minutes, liquidizing, and mixing in thin slices of raclette or Fontina and leaving them to melt.

➤ Serve roast chicken or game birds with a bunch of watercress at the side and some game chips or crisps.

See also:

Tomato, Watercress and Ginger Quiche (page 88)

Index